A Countryman's Flowers

A Countryman's Flowers

by Hal Borland ❧ photographs by Les Line

ALFRED A. KNOPF   NEW YORK   1981

For Barbara and for Lois

Contents

Foreword

Everyone should know something about the flowers that bloom around us. Enough to tell a violet from a primrose, at least, a hawkweed from a honeysuckle. Without flowers this would be a drab place indeed, and without their green leaves we would all soon be gasping for breath. The plants are the makers of this earth's atmospheric oxygen, and the source of all the food we eat, to boot—every animal on earth either eats plants directly or eats other animals that eat plants. So salute the green leaf and thank it for your life. Cherish the blossom, whose job it is to make the seeds that perpetuate the plants with those green leaves.

But flowers are interesting as well as vitally important. That is why when someone asks what are my favorite wildflowers, I always hesitate. I can't honestly say I have favorites. When we planned this book, I drew up a list of eighty or so that appealed to me simply because they were interesting. Some were beautiful in shape, some beautiful in color, though half the beauty, as always, is in the observer's eyes. Some I chose because of their unusual habits of growth or flowering. Some I included because of old tales and legends about them, not caring whether the tales were true or not. Some I chose because of the stories behind their names, or because their names have some special meaning.

Names are fascinating, and the names of flowering plants are full of history and imagination, not to mention the folk poetry in them. In the Book of Genesis we are told that Adam named "every living creature." Nothing is said about naming plants, but for a long time they had only the kind of names Adam, or more likely Eve, might have given them. Simple, descriptive, poetically picturesque names, such as blue-eyed grass, lady's-tresses, adder's mouth, butter flowers, lady's slipper. But eventually scholars tried to list the plants and found a confusion of names from place to place. Finally one of Aristotle's students, Theophrastus, tried his hand at it and compiled an herbal, a plant list, based on the most commonly used names. When the Romans succeeded the Greeks, they tried to improve the herbal by making the names descriptive. Eventually the names became so long that even the scholars couldn't understand them.

Meanwhile, the ordinary people went on using the common names. So did the herb dealers and herb doctors, who had more practical knowledge about plants than anyone else. This duality of names continued until 1735, when Carl Linnaeus, a young Swede, devised a simple, workable system of nomenclature based on Greek and Latin. Linnaeus gave us a precise international plant language that could be understood anywhere. But the old names persisted, and still do. Webster's unabridged dictionary lists more than a hundred and fifty *wort* names for plants still in use. *Wort* comes from the Old English *wyrt* and means plant or root. The herb folk simply tacked a descriptive word onto it—feverwort, for example, sometimes called horse gentian, and botanically *Triosteum perfoliatum*, was a plant from which the herb doctors brewed an infusion to reduce fevers. Sneezewort was supposed to stop sneezing, cankerwort was good to treat cankers, and fleawort may have helped rid a dog—or a person—of fleas.

So we still have this dual system, which overlaps at many points. The scientific names are specific. The common names are sometimes local or regional and therefore may vary from place to place. They persist because they are a part of the common language, they often are picturesque, and they have folk poetry in them.

I shall have more to say about names as we go along, and for convenience as well as for accuracy I have given both a common name and the scientific name for each entry—the common name as I know it, that is. My pokeweed may be your inkberry or even false hellebore, but botanically it is *Phytolacca americana* I am talking about, and by using the scientific name we can get together.

All the flowers in this book are familiar to me. I can find most of them within a mile of my own house here in the lower Berkshires of southern New England. A good many of them are ordinary weeds in many people's estimation—daisies, mustard, and bindweed, for example. But among the various definitions of the word *weed*, I think first of the one that says a weed is a plant that grows where you don't want it. Those miniature pansies we call Johnny-jump-ups have become a weed in our vegetable garden. And I have heard the ox-eye daisy called farmer's curse because it grows so freely in hayfields, where it's definitely a weed.

Actually, many of the wildflowers we know today were brought here from Europe as garden flowers, either for their beauty or their herbal virtues. One authority says that, of all the wildflowers in New England today, the only natives are milkweed, wild geranium or crane's-bill, robin's plantain, steeplebush, asters, and goldenrod. Even the black-eyed Susan, though native to America, came east from the grassy prairies of the West only after white settlement. The others apparently came from abroad, most of them with the first settlers—even the daisies, even the dandelions.

A few of this book's flowers may be hard to find. One must get one's feet wet to examine a marsh marigold or a cattail. And for some of them one must know someone who knows where to look. But most are roadside and meadow flowers, and a good many can be found on vacant lots in most cities. I have seen evening primroses growing from a crack in the pavement just beyond midtown in Manhattan; and if one goes down along the docks there, one can find many unexpected wildflowers rooted in the cracks and crannies.

This isn't intended to be a handbook or a guide. The botanical information is kept to a minimum, and I have tried to use few obscure scientific terms. For those who would know more about these flowers, excellent guides and handbooks are available.

The pictures in this book were taken by Les Line, the editor of *Audubon* magazine and one of the best nature photographers I know. Some of them, but by no means all, were taken here in my corner of New England, in my own pastures and woodland, down this country road, just beyond the next hill.

The entries are arranged somewhat by habitat. In the first section are a selection of those I find in what I consider my dooryard—around the house, on the lawn, back of the woodshed, along the garden fence, creeping into the vegetable garden itself. Then comes the section on the roadside, a country road used by the school bus, the milk tanker, the rural mail carrier, and maybe a dozen resident farm folk. Third is the old pasture, a grassy patch of valley land rising partway up the mountainside and fringed by trees. And, fourth, the brook and bog, a hollow where a small brook spills its water from the mountainside, and from which another brook trickles to the river.

A few words of caution perhaps should be added. Throughout the text I have spoken of how American Indians used many of these plants for medicinal purposes. I have also mentioned the use of them by English and colonial American herb doctors. This is in no sense an endorsement of such use. Some of the plants are acutely poisonous. Some have made their way into the pharmacopoeia of modern medicine, but far more of them have not. My advice is that you do not chew or eat the stems, leaves, berries, fruits, or roots of any plant you do not know, beyond a doubt, to be harmless, and that you do not drink any tea, essence, or infusion made from any part of a plant unknown to you.

On the other hand, do not feel that the plant world is forbidding and dangerous. I know of fewer than half a dozen plants poisonous to the touch, as is poison ivy, and perhaps two dozen that are poisonous to eat.

HAL BORLAND

A Countryman's Flowers

The Dooryard

Depending on how you look at it, we live in a wildflower garden or a weed patch. Our dooryard extends from the big old barn on one side to the vegetable garden on the other, from the home pasture in the back to the country road and the riverbank in front. I keep the grass around the house mowed, in season, for a lawn. The garden has a fence only theoretically rabbit-proof and woodchuck-proof; that fence is thickly twined with vines, and catbirds and cardinals nest there. Half a dozen old apple trees are huge bouquets, loud with bees, in the backyard each May.

Every March I begin to watch for spring in this dooryard. With luck, I find its first signs here in early April. Dandelions appear. Chickweed is in bloom. (Chickweed, of course, grows anywhere it can find root room and blooms almost every month of the year.) Gill-over-the-ground, with its small frilled leaves, appears, but it won't bloom till late April, and by then we will have lilacs and apple blossoms. We will also have plantain out by the garage, to feed the woolly-bear caterpillars that hibernated in the garage and now will turn into pretty pink and white moths. Back of the garage the bur marigolds will be up and thriving; they blew in from somewhere a few years ago, and I can't seem to discourage them. I content myself by saying I'd rather have them there than in front of the house.

Behind the woodshed is a tangle of wild raspberries, nettles, star-of-Bethlehem, dock, and, of all things, big violets. Violets seem to like our soil. They grow everywhere—in the middle of the lawn, in the garden path, among the carrots, under the bridal-wreath bush, in the lily-of-the-valley bed.

Out beside the old barn is a sampling of many crops that have been stored there, plus the wildlings that grow with them in the hay-fields. Alfalfa, of course, and timothy grass. But also goldenrod of half a dozen species, daisies, pasture thistles, black-eyed Susans, Canada hawkweed, winter cress, field mustard. We keep the barn-yard mowed, but these wildlings persist around the barn in a kind of choker necklace that the mower can't quite reach.

The real collection of wildlings, however, is along the garden fence and in the garden itself. Many of them are, technically, "escapes," plants that once were grown and tended as flowers or herbs but then went wild. And here they are, doing their best to get back. The campions line the fence. The bindweed—I prefer to call it a wild morning glory—twines on the fence and anything else handy, even the sage in the herb bed. Several big pokeweed plants persist just outside the fence. And inside, along and between the rows, are chickweed, purslane, galinsoga, gill, spiderwort. I some-times look at my vegetable garden and wonder that it produces any vegetables at all. We till the soil, we plant, we weed, eventually we pluck, and we get all we really need from the garden. Yet we resent those plants which we don't eat. Why? It's human nature, I sup-pose. We have to run things, be the boss.

But I am the observer, in March and April. I watch for spring. I gloat over summer here in the dooryard, even admire the burdock blossoms and the thistles. In the autumn I watch for the big clump of New England asters, the deep purple ones with rich golden cen-ters, to bloom along the garden fence at the far end where it borders the home pasture. The asters come to bloom and I feel that we have royalty among us. I know that our dooryard is a special place and that we have been privileged to enjoy it for another year.

Common Blue Violet

VIOLA PAPILIONACEA

Gray lists fifty-one species of violets, which range in color from white through yellow and the whole span of lavenders, blues, and purples. Some of them can be found virtually everywhere in the United States. This one, which has no name beyond common blue violet, prefers damp places but will grow on stony hillsides if there is shade. On dry ground its leaf stems are longer than its flower stems, so one has to look to find the blossoms. But in damp soil the flowers reach up beyond the leaves and occasionally make a purple canopy for the plant. The color varies somewhat with the soil and the sunlight. I have found them very deep velvety purple and again quite light blue.

All violets cross with each other, absolutely wanton. Bees do most of the pollinating, and they make no distinction between species, so there are hybrids by the score. In our garden we had natives, mostly the common blue violets pictured here but also the bigger swamp violets. Then someone gave us a couple of white violet plants, which we set in the ground. A few years later we had all kinds of violets everywhere—whites, whites striped with purple, big purples, small blues. And they are still crossing. We find new variations every year.

The old herbalists used violets, especially the flowers, to make concoctions for all kinds of inflammations and for hoarseness. The Indians used powdered violet root as an emetic, and the flowers were decocted for a laxative. They also used violet tea for lung diseases and respiratory troubles. And they believed it induced sleep.

4

Field Chickweed

CERASTIUM ARVENSE

Don't get involved with the chickweeds. There are so many of them that you can easily get lost trying to run down the name of any particular one. Besides, as flowers they are in no sense spectacular. Some of them do have a remarkable hardiness—here, in this New England climate, I have found chickweed in bloom eleven months of the year. If I had looked harder, I might even have found it in bloom in January. This was the common chickweed, *Stellaria media*, the one most widely distributed. It has very small white flowers and its white petals are split down the middle, making them look like ten instead of five.

The one we have here, however, has a flower big enough to notice and really is quite handsome. It grows as much as a foot high, has the typical long, narrow leaves clasping the stem, and insists on growing in cultivated ground. That *arvense* in the botanical name means "of the cultivated ground." If you know the garden flower lychnis, look for a blossom something like that when you search for field chickweed. But the chickweed foliage is bright green, not silvery.

Chickweed is edible, but I never heard of anyone eating it in salad or boiled as a green. The old herbals seem to have no use for it. But American Indians gathered it, leaf and stem, and pounded it into a poultice for ulcers. Apparently it had some good effect, for it was rather widely used among the Indians.

Heal-All

P R U N E L L A   V U L G A R I S

Here is a weedy little plant that is found everywhere, all across America and in most of the other countries of the world, and yet never seems to become a real pest. It doesn't take over a lawn or even a roadside. It grows in individual plants and sends up its flower heads, which are rather fat clusters of mint flowers, purplish and violet in color, occasionally white. Mow it down with the grass and it will send up another flower head, and another. It doesn't crowd out the grass, as do dandelions. It merely persists.

Heal-all, or Selfheal as it is sometimes called, is a member of the mint family. But despite the common name, it never was used as an elixir or a cure-all. It is also sometimes called carpenter weed, for reasons I cannot discover. It does have the square stem typical of the mint family, but surely that isn't enough to justify such a name.

Actually, the botanical name tells more about the plant than any of the common names, and even that is distorted. In Germany the plant was used to treat the severe throat inflammation known as quinsy, which is called *braune* in German. In German the plant was called *brunella*. Linnaeus, a Swede, seems to have misheard the German name and set it down as *prunella*, and there it is in the botany lists, *Prunella*, a plant whose leaves were bruised and bound on sore throats of people suffering from quinsy.

American Indians used the plant for sore throat and diarrhea, especially in babies.

8

Tall Sunflower

HELIANTHUS GIGANTEUS

Indian sun and golden flower of Peru are other names that have been used for the sunflowers we know. They may well have originated in Peru, but they have been growing here in North America for a long, long time. Kansas sunflowers, some call them, though the most common roadside sunflower in Kansas is a shorter species with heart-shaped leaves, *Helianthus annuus*. The one we speak of here grows as much as twelve feet tall, has lance-shaped leaves, the upper ones quite stemless, and flowers only about two inches broad. The petals usually number fewer than twenty and are a bright yellow. The centers are a dull yellow but darken as they mature.

The sunflowers growing on the High Plains of present-day Oklahoma and Kansas amazed the early Spanish explorers, particularly the Coronado party which went searching for the fabled cities of gold. Toward the end of that disillusioning journey the leaders were saying that the only gold they found was in the petals of flowers growing on weeds.

French explorers found the Indians along Lake Huron growing sunflowers that they said grew twenty feet high and had flower heads a foot across. I can believe this. We have grown, in our own garden, sunflowers that were eighteen feet tall and had heads a foot across.

The Indians ate sunflower seeds, raw and parched, and made a coffee-like drink from them. They even boiled the seeds to extract oil to grease their hair—the same sunflower oil we use today in margarine. The English herbalists were baffled by the sunflower, but Gerard found that the buds, boiled and buttered, were "exceeding pleasant meat," something like artichokes.

Asteraceae

Common Burdock

ARCTIUM MINUS

The common name may come from either the plant's prickly burs or the botanical name, which is from *arctos*, a bear, referring to the rough, forbidding fruit or burs. The "dock" part comes from an old Anglo-Saxon word *docce*, meaning one of the plants we still call dock. But burdock is unrelated to the true docks, which are akin to buckwheat.

Burdock grows almost anywhere and can become a huge plant, six feet high, with big leaves spreading over a circle seven or eight feet across. It has rather pretty purple flowers, but it's really distinguished by those burs that come after the flowers. They are an inch or more long, egg-shaped, and covered with hooked spines. They can catch on anything, it seems, and a dog that runs through a burdock patch when the burs are ripe can carry home a load of thorny capsules that will take his owner hours to remove.

A biennial, burdock builds a big root the first year, then dies after the second year's crop of flowers and burs. That first-year root is rich with herbal medicines, which were used chiefly by the Indians and the early American herb doctors to soothe sciatica, rheumatism, and gout. It was made into a salve with which to treat wounds, and it was used as a wash for burns and skin irritations. It was also used as a diuretic and a tonic. In fact, whenever one had an ache or a pain, it usually was a safe bet to dig a burdock root and make a salve or a tea. It nearly always helped. Some people, not the Indians, occasionally ate the stalks of burdock, first stripping off the outer rind. It is said to taste like asparagus when boiled and buttered. But it is also very laxative.

Asteraceae

Common Dandelion

TARAXACUM OFFICINALE

Dandelions, of one species or another, grow virtually all over the world. The common name comes from the French *dent-de-lion,* "tooth of the lion," and refers to the tooth-edged leaves. Dandelion yellow is traditional, a bright, clear color.

Dandelions have been grown as flowers, from time to time, and as herbs. But in most places they are weeds. In my area they have invaded gardens, lawns, and hayfields in such numbers that they have almost dispossessed the grass. I keep our lawn relatively clear of them only by constant effort, because the seeds blow in from every direction, and dandelion seeds seem to be especially fertile.

Even though it has become a pest, the dandelion has much to be said for it. Its young leaves have been eaten, raw or boiled, ever since people began cooking. I am no particular partisan of dandelion greens, but they must be good for you. Anything that tastes that way *has* to be beneficial. The roots are bitter and astringent and were long used as an ingredient of spring tonic and blood purifiers. White settlers brewed a concoction from the roots, then laced it with gin. The Indians, originally lacking the gin, took it neat and seemed to get just as much benefit from it.

When I was young, we boys used the long, hollow flower stems as Pan-pipes, played long one-note sonatas on them. The bitter, milky juice puckered our mouths. Some people gathered that juice and let it jell a bit, then chewed it like gum. We never did. Sometimes we made elaborate curls from those stems by simply splitting them, and used them as fright-wigs. We plucked ripe heads and saw how many tufts we could blow away with one breath. We loved dandelions.

16

Pokeweed

PHYTOLACCA AMERICANA

The botanical name for this plant is one of those bastard words we find in botany, from the Greek *phyton,* for plant, and the Latin *lacca,* crimson-lake, a shade of red, for the crimson color of the juice from the berries. It may have some reference also to the red stems of the plant. The common names are myriad: Indian poke, skoke, inkberry, pigeon berry, cancer jalap, pocan, American nightshade, etc.

Poke is one of the few plants that bear blossoms, green berries, and ripe berries all at the same time. It grows very large, with a central stalk as much as four inches in diameter and branches like a tree. All this from a root that seems to grow bigger each year. The plant dies down every autumn. I have dug up poke plants year after year, trying to get rid of them at the edge of the garden; but I always miss some part of the root, so a brand new poke plant appears and starts all over again. The flowers are small and greenish-white. They come in long racemes and ripen into purple-black berries full of seeds. The juice from the ripe berries was once used for ink. It makes an almost indelible stain on clothing.

The young leaves of poke, which appear in early spring, are a traditional spring green, boiled like spinach. The leaves and the berries both have a poisonous element in them which apparently is neutralized by cooking. I once wrote that the berries are dangerously poisonous to people, although birds eat them, and I got a sheaf of letters from people who told me they had eaten pokeberry pudding and pie for years. But if you want to eat pokeberry greens, I strongly advise you to cook them first.

Phytolaccaceae

Hedge Bindweed

CONVOLVULUS SEPIUM

Bindweeds are morning glories. We plant tame morning glories beside the woodshed and set strings for them to climb. Bindweeds plant themselves along the garden fence and climb all over it (even though we try to discourage them) and make the mornings pretty with their trumpets, sometimes pink, other times white. Besides, bindweeds are cousins of sweet potatoes, which alone gives them status in my eyes.

These climbers grow swiftly, and they curl their stems around any support they can find, a string, a wire, a grass stem, the flower stems of the day-lilies at the roadside. Here in the northern hemisphere they twine to the right, clockwise. In the southern hemisphere, I am told, such climbing vines twine to the left, counterclockwise. Why this should be so, I do not know, though I have heard it is because of Earth's rotation on its axis. I have to take this on faith.

There are a number of morning glories growing wild, including one that creates a huge root, big as a man's leg, five or six feet underground, from which it sends up shoots year after year. But most of them are more conventional plants that grow from seed and die every autumn. The flowers on all of them open early in the morning, around sunrise, and close by noon. It is fascinating to watch a morning glory unfurl itself, twisting out of its bud and opening its trumpet like a silken tube—but you have to get up early to see this happen.

The Indians of the West made an infusion of bindweed leaves and used it for heart trouble. I have never heard of any other use for the plant.

Common Strawberry

FRAGARIA VIRGINIANA

There is a legend about a young Indian and his squaw who quarreled and she ran away. He followed but couldn't catch her until she saw a patch of wild strawberries full of ripe fruit. She was unable to resist the berries, stopped, plucked, ate, and was all sweet and loving when her mate arrived. She fed him a handful, and life was good again for both of them.

I can almost believe it. When wild strawberries are ripe, in June, I don't know of any fruit that surpasses them. And that probably has something to do with my admiration for the three-part leaves and gleaming white blossoms of the plant. As a boy I knew the species common in the West, called the wood strawberry, *Fragaria vesca*. It is a stocky plant, and its berries are bigger than those of the eastern species. Otherwise they are almost identical, leaf and blossom. The botanical name, *Fragaria*, comes from the Latin *fragra*, meaning fragrant, and refers to the unmistakable sweetness of the fruit.

The early English didn't think too much of strawberries; they were such a chore to pick. But they were served on the royal table. An expense account of Henry VIII speaks of "small basket strawberries, 10 pence." That was in 1530. American Indians, on the other hand, thought strawberries were a special treat, ate all they could pick, even made a "soup" or sauce of them. One account says they sweetened them "with early morning dew shaken from milkweed blossoms," but that is a bit too poetic. Anyway, wild strawberries need no sweetening.

Rosaceae

Dock

RUMEX

Docks are common weeds throughout the United States. They bear loose clusters of greenish little flowers of no real consequence, which ripen into winged seeds, heart-shaped in outline. The seeds actually look like miniature buckwheat kernels, and the plants belong to the buckwheat family. The seed heads are more eye-catching and interesting than the flowers.

All the various docks have been used in herbal medicine and as pot herbs. As a pot herb, dock was boiled with almost any other green—dandelions, poke, mustard. The Indians also used it as a meat tenderizer. Its sour content, oxalic acid, went to work on the meat when a few dock leaves were put in the pot. Indians also used dried dock leaves as a tobacco substitute, but I can attest that it doesn't rank high in that category. The root, however, was used as a tonic and a laxative; and I wonder why so many of those old herbal remedies were both laxative and tonic, or if the two were almost synonymous in those days. Some pioneers also dried the roots, ground them, and used the powder for a dentifrice. It probably puckered the mouth, maybe made it feel clean.

An English acquaintance tells me that as a boy in England he and his playmates used dock leaves to cool and ease the sting of nettles. They simply plucked a big dock leaf and held it on the nettled spot, and soon the stinging eased and disappeared.

Gill-over-the-Ground

GLECHOMA HEDERACEA

If gill-over-the-ground, also called ground ivy, were not so plentiful, and hence so much a weed, it would rate as a choice ground cover with modest but beautiful, small violet-blue flowers. It comes to full blossom in May and grows almost everywhere, trailing over the ground like true ivy, though it actually is a mint. Its small, scalloped, heart-shaped leaves have a mild mint tang. Its flowers follow the tubular mint pattern.

Like many other mints, gill-over-the-ground came from England. Some people say that the early settlers brought it to the New World for its blossoms as a reminder of English spring, that it was their equivalent of America's trailing arbutus. Others claim it was brought here for use in making ale and beer, and this seems more likely than the spring-flower story.

In England the plant was known as ale-hoof. The "hoof" part was an old word meaning to inflate, probably as yeast inflates bread dough or mash. The "gill" in the name is said to come from the French or Norman, *guiller*, and refers to its use in brewing. Apparently it had some of the same quality that hops did but was easier to grow. Hence the early colonists brought it along, having no idea it would leap their garden walls and take to the fields. But that is what happened. And now gill-over-the-ground is one of the wildlings, a fugitive trying tirelessly to get back into the garden, where it is a weed. A prodigal, in a sense, but independent and prosperous.

lamiaceae

Star-of-Bethlehem

ORNITHOGALUM UMBELLATUM

I never knew star-of-Bethlehem to grow in the wild until a friend gave us a clump of evening primroses that had a couple of star bulbs in it somewhere. They grew and multiplied, wandered all over the flower garden, got into the vegetable garden, crossed the road, and took off down the riverbank. Now I find them a quarter of a mile from the house, and they are still going. Each year I have to thin them out in the garden, and it seems that every one I throw away takes root somewhere. Besides this, they seem to produce good seed and quite a bit of it. I suspect the ants of carrying that seed from one place to another, though I have no idea whether or not they eat it. I shouldn't be surprised if the chipmunks also carry it about, and they probably eat it, too—they eat all kinds of unexpected things. Anyway, the star-of-Bethlehem has gone vigorously wild here, as it goes wild in many places.

It is a rather pretty little flower, with long, slender leaves and white petals that have green on their outer sides. The blossoms are borne in a cluster at the tip of a flower stalk, which grows ten or twelve inches tall.

Some people, I have been told, call this flower nap-at-noon, though on sunny days the blossoms stay open right through the noon hour. They remain closed on cloudy days and at night. The botanical name is from the Greek words for bird's milk, probably a whimsical way of saying the plant has milky white flowers.

Bladder Campion

SILENE CUCUBALUS

The campions are pinks, second cousins of the spice pinks of the flower garden, and in Elizabethan England the pinks were called gillofloures. *Gerard's Herball* said that a conserve made of "Clove Gillofloures and sugar" was "exceeding cordiall and doth comfort the heart." So far as I know, nobody ever made a conserve of campions, but it, too, might comfort the heart.

Another common name for bladder campion is maiden's tears. Big tears, I must say, for the fat, inflated bladder likened to tears is a full half-inch in diameter. It looks like a miniature melon, light green with dark green veining, and from its top spring the white petals, five of them, each so deeply cut that they appear to be ten. The plant commonly grows eighteen inches tall, sometimes twice that, and bears the flowers in clusters at the tip of the stems. The long, narrow leaves come in pairs, opposite each other, and clasp the stem.

Another name for this and all campions is catchfly, and that, like the family name, *Silene,* goes back to the legends about Silenus, the foster father of Bacchus. Silenus also was quite a toper, it seems, and from time to time was found in a stupor, his face covered with beery foam. Some of the campions have sticky secretions that look vaguely like such foam. Flies like the taste and occasionally are trapped in it.

Bladder campion grows vigorously along our garden fence, trying to get a foothold inside. It also grows at many rural roadsides.

Caryophyllaceae

The Roadside

When we first came here, more than twenty-five years ago, ours was an unpaved country road left over from horse-and-wagon days. It wound up the valley, following the natural contours, along the river, across the meadows, over the rocky outcrops, through the damp swales. In spring it was hub-deep in mud. In winter it was drifted full of snow. Soon after we arrived, however, the township graded, graveled, and oiled the road and eventually black-topped it. It was made passable the year around. But, as with all its back roads, the town continued to mow the roadsides twice a season instead of spraying with herbicides. So we still have a luxurious growth of native wildlings. For years I have walked this road at all seasons, listened to its birds, watched its animals, witnessed its budding, its blossoming, and its ripening. It is more than a road; it is a cross-section of the countryside.

One of the earliest roadside plants to show signs of life is celandine, a humble member of the poppy clan. Its bright green leaves often appear before the snow is gone, and its small yellow flowers frequently open while the bloodroot is in bloom. Bloodroot is another member of the poppy family, and it also grows in colonies along the road in dampish places. When bloodroot blooms, we go to the roadside to pick a mess of winter cress for early spring greens. There, too, we cut fresh, new shoots of milkweed, which we eat as a stand-in for asparagus. And there I always find the fresh, new stalks of giant mulleins starting their astonishing reach toward the sun from last year's faded, rumpled rosette of fuzzy leaves.

Once spring is really under way, you can't keep up with the

roadside. The meadow's flowers grow there, and the hilltop's flowers. Columbines will be in bloom in certain places along the road in early May. All the clovers will be there, and alfalfa to boot. Solomon's seal will be found in June. And daisies and black-eyed Susans, more than you can count. Some years it will be white with Queen Anne's lace. Some years it will come into September white and pink with bouncing Bet.

And meanwhile the evening primroses will open their bright yellow blossoms every afternoon when the sun is halfway down the western sky. The milkweed will come to tufts of blossoms fragrant as tuberoses and actually smelling much like them. Bittersweet will climb the trees and shrubs. Wild cucumber will drape the bushes with its bright green, star-shaped leaves and small white blooms. Virgin's bower, the wild clematis, will climb with the other vines, open its countless small white blossoms, and slowly mature toward the old-age stage of autumn, when it is aptly called old man's beard.

If you would know any area's wild plants, find a rural road that winds through the hills. Park your car. Get out and walk, with your eyes open and your senses alert. You will hear birds that you haven't heard for months, maybe years. You may see dragonflies, butterflies, beetles you had long forgotten. And you certainly will find a sampling of the flowers that grow on the nearby hills and in the valleys where brooks flow and frogs trill at night. In spring you will see May approaching, May and violets. In summer you will hear the cicada shrilling the message of late July and early August and see the first spray of goldenrod. In September you will see more asters than you can count, and you will have the maple trees, the ash, the aspens, the wild cherries, in all their fall array, for a bonus.

False Solomon's Seal

SMILACINA RACEMOSA

This one is also called false spikenard, or Solomon's zigzag. It is easily distinguished from true Solomon's seal by its zigzag stem, which seems to veer at every leaf. It also has all its blossoms at the tip, in a loose panicle instead of two at a time at the base of the leaves. And in September its berries form a loose cluster at the tip, first green, then yellowish with madder brown speckles, then a dull deep red that looks almost translucent. They are not poisonous, but not very tasty either.

American Indians used these berries as a cathartic. A few of them provide only a somewhat bitter, somewhat aromatic taste, but a handful of them can act as a purgative. The Indians had other cathartics, however, and used the plant primarily for its rootstock, which is rather large. They dug and roasted these rootstocks and ate them as a vegetable. The rootstocks taste something like tame parsnips, and they are rich in starch, a good addition to the outdoor diet.

Botanically, this plant belongs to the big lily family, but so does asparagus, and so do the trilliums. So does smilax, or catbrier, for that matter. And yet false Solomon's seal, *Smilacina* to the botanists, is only a very distant cousin of the smilaxes.

This one blooms at about the same time as the true Solomon's seal, or somewhat earlier. I have known people to mistake it, when in bloom, for one of the baneberries, though there is no resemblance at all in the leaves. The tufts of white bloom are vaguely alike, though the baneberry bloom is more of a rounded puff, the false Solomon's seal bloom a looser, more conical shape.

Polygonaceæ

Rough-Fruited Cinquefoil

POTENTILLA RECTA

Cinquefoil simply means five-leaf, and the botanical *Potentilla* comes from *potent*, because the plant was reputed to have strong medicinal powers. There are about a dozen common species. I prefer this one because its flowers are such a beautifully clean light yellow. The plant grows about two feet tall and likes good soil but is not really choosy. I find it on roadsides and around village dumps as well as in the borders of my pastures and occasionally in my garden.

English herbalists recommended boiling cinquefoil roots in wine as a treatment for gout—externally. A decoction of the roots in water was also recommended for toothache: "Held in the moth it doth mitigate the paine of the teeth." There were other uses, however. In *The Art of Simpling*, written in 1657, Coles said, "The ointment witches use is made of the fat of children dug up from their graves and mixed with the juice of smallage, Wolfsbane and cinquefoil and fine wheat flour."

The American Indians were less macabre. They brewed a decoction of cinquefoil leaves and stems to use as an astringent and a cooling agent for fevers and infections. A decoction of the bark soothed inflamed eyes. Powdered bark was used for various troubles, from nosebleed to kidney ulcers. And the Indians, like the English, used it for toothache; they boiled the roots and held them in the mouth.

All but one of the cinquefoils I know are yellow-flowered. That one, marsh cinquefoil, is purple. They all belong to the rose family, are cousins of the apple, the raspberry, and the strawberry.

Rosaceae

Rabbit's-Foot Clover

TRIFOLIUM ARVENSE

Some call this stone clover, because it will grow in stony ground. But those fuzzy flower heads, pinkish-gray in color, look enough like the hairy feet of small rabbits to justify the rabbit's-foot name. It grows only twelve inches high, at most. Its light green leaves, threefold in the clover pattern, are long, narrow, and blunt-pointed. The flowers are sweet-scented, though not obtrusively so, and honeybees love them. The plant is commonly regarded as a weed, though not really bothersome. Livestock eat it, and it grows in almost any soil, in old fields, at roadsides, just about anywhere, from coast to coast and from Canada to the Gulf. Where I live, it comes to bloom in May, usually late May.

There are many species of clover growing wild in the United States, and all are important sources of food for birds, bees, and animals. They are good for people, too, having a high protein content. The American Indians have been eating clover since the mountains were young, either raw or cooked like any other green. A special spring treat would be a mess of boiled clover heads. I have never tasted them, but they should be good fare at anyone's table.

This little rabbit's-foot clover is almost pretty enough to pluck and bring into the house. Combine it with the little yellow hop clover, which often grows in the same area, and it becomes quite decorative. Both the rabbit's-foot and hop clover are annuals, growing from seed every year. That is one reason they spread so fast and can vanish so quickly from a particular area.

Fabaceae

Red Clover

TRIFOLIUM PRATENSE

This is the common roadside and field clover of America. It is grown as pasturage and for hay, but it takes off on its own so that we find it practically anywhere. Its big leaves, three—rarely four—to a stem, each with a white or light green triangle marked on its upper surface, are unmistakable. Its blossoms are big and showy, usually crimson or magenta. And usually those blossoms have bumblebees on them or nearby. Only bumblebees can pollinate the flowers satisfactorily.

When clover was first introduced into Australia, which does not have it as a native, the clover grew well but soon died out. It never formed fertile seeds. Finally someone thought of the bumblebees, took some to Australia, and thereafter the clover throve and renewed itself. The florets in the head of bloom have plenty of nectar, but they are so deep that ordinary bees cannot reach it. And butterflies, though they have long tongues, are too light to push down the keel of the floret and expose the anthers. Only the big, burly bumblebees can open the florets, get the nectar, and at the same time cross-pollinate the florets. The well-known clover honey that comes to our table is made from the smaller florets of white clover, which the honeybees can open easily.

The Indians brewed a tea from red clover blossoms, which they believed cleansed their blood. The same tea mixed with the juice of roasted onions and strained honey was good for coughs and was occasionally used as a salve—a sticky one, I would say—for sores. An infusion of red clover also was used to calm the spasms of whooping cough.

Fabaceae

Common St. John's-Wort

HYPERICUM PERFORATUM

Besides the deep golden yellow of its blossoms, which are very handsome, there are two fascinating characteristics of common St. John's-wort. One is the row of tiny black dots along the edges of the flower's petals, making them look as if they'd been hemmed by a skillful seamstress. The other is the row of semi-transparent spots along the edges of the small elliptical leaves, which make them look like oddly windowed little boats.

There are a dozen species in the St. John's-wort family, from a marshland creeper to an upland shrub, but this one is a rather bushy, much-branched perennial that is found in old pastures, on roadsides, and on dry, gravelly hillsides. It grows almost all over the United States, and it has a variety of common names, all regional —Tipton-weed, Klamath-weed, goatweed, Eola-weed, amberweed, rosin rose.

The Indians used a decoction of leaves and flowers as an astringent and boiled the plant to use as a poultice for wounds and swellings. The white pioneers and herb doctors tried, then rejected it. But the old English herbalists thought a good deal of it. I like this recipe from *Gerard's Herball*:

"The leaves, floures, and seeds, stamped, and put into a glasse with white wine, oile olive, oile of Turpentine, and set in the sun eight or ten daies, and then strained from those herbs and a like quantity of new put in and sunned in like manner, doth make an oile of the colour of bloud which is most pretious remedie for deep wounds. Or any wound made with a venomous weapon."

42

Purple Loosestrife

L Y T H R U M   S A L I C A R I A

Here is a good example of the confusion that can come from using only common names for plants. There are two groups of loose-strifes. One belongs to the primrose family; the other has its own family, the loosestrifes. Even the handbooks list them both as loose-strifes. The one in the primrose family is, botanically, *Lysimachia*, and the one we are talking about here is botanically *Lythrum*. Yet both are called willow-herb at times, and even long purples. Quite confusing.

Anyway, here is *Lythrum salicaria*, often called purple loosestrife. It is a tall, slender, many-branched perennial with six-petaled blos-soms, purple or magenta in color, in long terminal spikes. The flow-ers are fertilized by honeybees and bumblebees, and probably by various butterflies, which are steady patrons at their pollen sup-plies. I think those butterflies add greatly to the beauty of the flowers, which are in no sense eye-catching. The other loosestrife, the *Lysimachia*, has yellow flowers and five petals, not six, borne in very loose clusters.

The old herbals speak of this purple loosestrife as "a bastard kind" and seem to link it with the one that belongs to the evening primrose family. Gerard said that the smoke from burned loose-strife "driveth away serpents, and killeth flies and gnats in a house." Beyond that, there wasn't much use for the plant.

The botanical name *Lythrum* comes from a name used by Dios-corides for a similar plant. The *salicaria* means willowlike and refers to the shape of the leaves, which resemble those of a weeping willow.

Lythraceae

Evening Primrose

OENOTHERA BIENNIS

Some of the most beautiful yellows to be found anywhere are on the evening primroses, especially in June. Or in those close cousins called sundrops. They are hot-weather flowers and are so adaptable that they grow almost anywhere, in fields or at roadsides, east of the Rocky Mountains.

These primroses are not to be confused with the primulas, to which they are no kin. They are members of the botanical family *Oenothera*, and they are native to America. Some varieties have been tamed and taken over by gardeners. They are often called four o'clocks, because they open late in the day. But here we speak of the wildlings.

The evening primrose is a sturdy plant that on occasion grows six feet tall, though more often it is only half that. It bears a generous handful of flowers at the tip on short stems rising from the bases of the upper leaves. These flowers are sometimes two inches across, but they last only one day. They shun full sunlight, opening toward dusk. Their opening is a marvel to watch, for they can unfurl completely in a minute or two. They are hosts to evening moths, the big ones, which do the pollinating.

The sundrops are somewhat smaller, both in plant and flower, but otherwise much the same as the tall primroses. And they, too, have that magnificent color.

In the plains country of the West and Southwest there is still another variety, small in plant but big in flower, sometimes four inches across, truly magnificent.

open late mday
4 o'clocks

NATIVE   Onagraceae

Common Milkweed

A S C L E P I A S   S Y R I A C A

Milkweed's fragrance is one of the sweetest of floral odors and reminds me of that from a tuberose. The flowers themselves are complex and bloom in large clusters; those of most milkweeds are a pale brownish-lilac in color, or sometimes a pale pinkish-crimson. They are so shaped that insects often are caught in them, by one leg, and are held until they die. The fertilized blossoms, as nearly everyone knows, form those rather large pods shaped something like a duck's head, which open in October and scatter silk-tufted seeds to the wind.

Milkweeds have challenged chemists and thread-makers for years. They milky sap can be made to yield a kind of rubber, but the process is too expensive to be profitable, and the quality of the rubber is doubtful. Thomas A. Edison is said to have worked at one time on a milkweed-rubber project, but he gave it up as impractical. And the floss attached to the seeds is long-fibered and silky, so much so that it has repeatedly tempted spinners who tried to make usable thread or yarn from it. But it lacks the natural twist needed for spinning. The only really practical use I know of for the plant is as a cooked green. We cut the young shoots before the first leaves have opened, cook them like asparagus, and find them delicious when buttered and lightly salted.

Pioneers used milkweed stalks, steeped, for an emetic, a cathartic, and an expectorant. The milky sap was said to remove wens and warts, and even corns from the feet. The Indians used the seeds, boiled, to draw out the poison of rattlesnake bites.

Asclepiadaceae

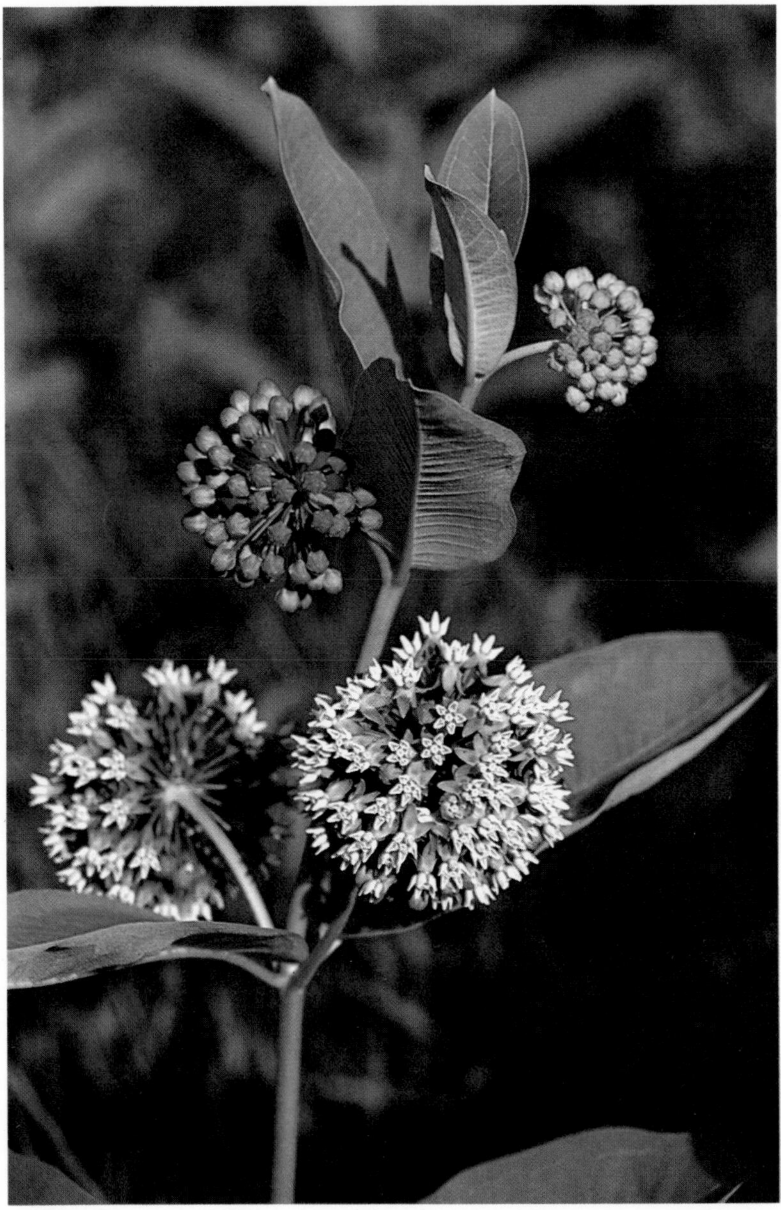

Bittersweet

CELASTRUS SCANDENS

Mention bittersweet and your listener may very well think of night-shade, *Solanum*, which is also called bittersweet, again pointing to that confusion of common names. But the bittersweet we are dealing with here is the climbing vine with the tiny, greenish-white five-petaled flowers that become those beautiful red-orange berries in the autumn, berries that are fully revealed only when the tan outer husk splits and curls back.

This bittersweet is sought by florists and visitors to the country in October, to use as a decorative element in autumn flower arrangements or to make a dry bouquet for winter. In good years it will be found twining up bushes and trees along almost every watercourse back in the hills. Although the blossoms are bisexual and all plants should bear fruit, every year I find a few plants with no fruit at all on them. I offer no explanation.

As a vine, bittersweet climbs by clinging, by twining round and round. Give it a tall weed or a young tree and it will climb to the top and wave around for something higher. If it happens to sprout beside a sapling, it will soon wrap itself around the young tree and establish itself there, never loosening its hug. Here in my study I have a length of gray birch that was hugged to death this way. It is about two inches through at the base, and the groove made by the twining bittersweet is half an inch deep all the way up, like a wide screw thread. The tree was dead when I found it, but the bitter-sweet vine was thriving.

50

Wild Bergamot

MONARDA FISTULOSA

Some people call this horse mint, which indicates that it does belong to the mint family. Others know it as Oswego tea, though more often the scarlet-flowered species is called that. And still others speak of it as beebalm, a name also used for the scarlet flower.

This is the one with a lavender blossom—or a purple, or a magenta, or even a pink blossom; the variation in color is quite wide and seems to depend on soil, climate, general growing conditions. In my area it is a pinkish-lavender, rather washed-out color. But still tousle-headed, full of that typical bergamot scent, and priceless to bees.

That bergamot scent, by the way, gave the plant its common name, in a roundabout way. In Turkish there is a term, *beg-armudi*, meaning literally "the prince's pear." It is the name of a special Turkish pear. From there, the name was taken over by a pear-shaped little orange, *Citrus bergamia*, that grows in Italy. The rind of the orange yields an oil used in perfumery, and it is primarily for the oil that the fruit is grown. However, the plant we are discussing here has an oil in its leaves and stems that has the same odor as the oil from the rind of the little orange, *Citrus bergamia*. So the plant got its name, bergamot, from a Turkish pear. Its botanical name simply honors a sixteenth-century Spanish physician-botanist, Nicholas Monardes.

Butter-and-Eggs

LINARIA VULGARIS

These little wild snapdragons grow virtually everywhere, north, south, east, west, country, suburb, city. Give them a bit of root room, a touch of moisture, and a little sunlight, and they grow eagerly, come to blossom by July, light yellow and bright orange combined, and continue in bloom till frost comes. Some know them as toadflax.

They grow along my country road, and in midsummer I often walk there just to see the butterflies that visit them. The yellow sulphurs, particularly, are nearly always there, and so are the Baltimores, which are black marked with red and pale yellow. Mingle the two species of butterflies around these little yellow and orange snapdragons and there is a lively swirl of roadside color. Those black Baltimore butterflies, by the way, lay their eggs on the figworts, the family to which butter-and-eggs belongs, and the dark orange and black caterpillars feed on the host plants in late summer.

Youngsters used to delight in picking butter-and-eggs, not for bouquets but for the fun of squeezing the individual blossoms and making them open and close their mouths, just like dragons. The flowers are about an inch long, including the long, slender spurs, and the plants bloom generously. The botanical name, *Linaria*, means flax, or linen, and refers to the plant's long, linear leaves, which are something like those of the flax plant. *Vulgaris* simply means that it is common—too common to be recognized as anything but a weed.

Scroph - now plantaginaceae

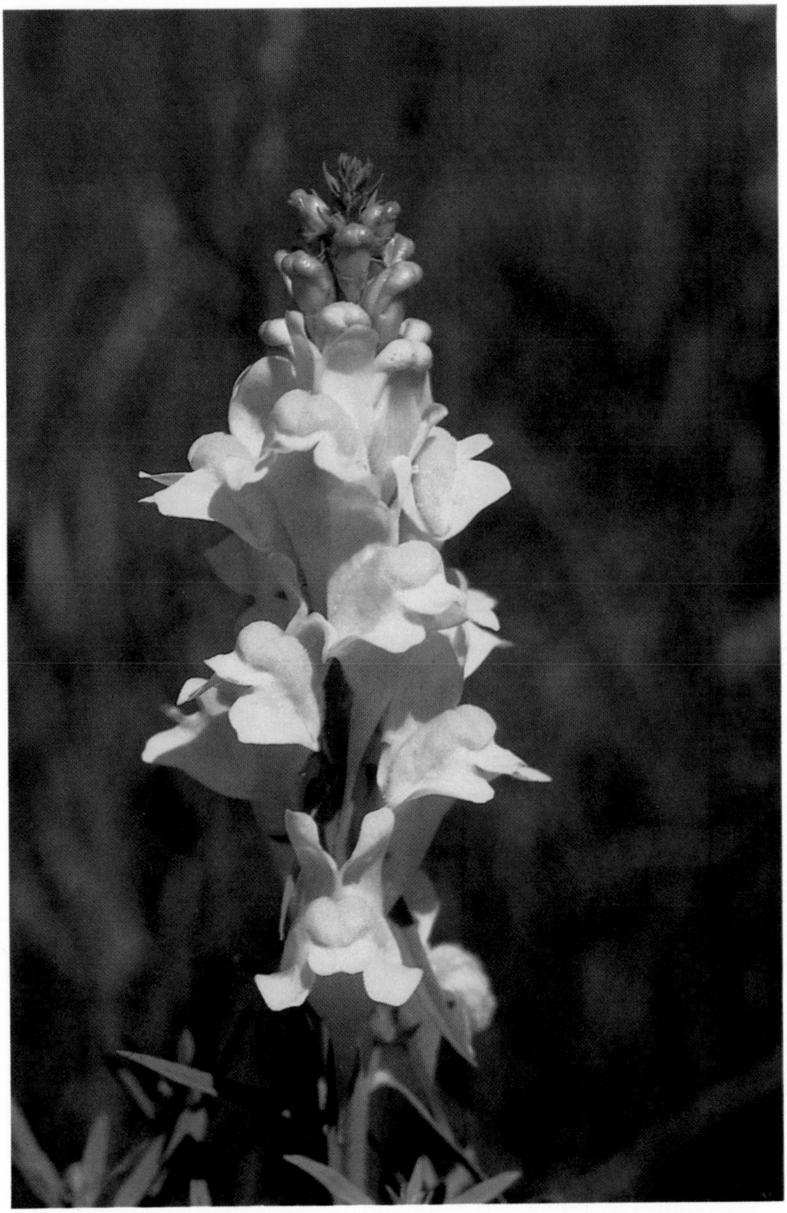

New England Aster

A S T E R   N O V A E - A N G L I A E

Here and there quite a few asters come to blossom in August, but the big purple asters belong to September, with a measure of overlap into October. They are the New England asters, both in common name and in Latin; and although they grow as far south as the Carolinas, they are a special autumn glory of the Northeast. They seem to achieve a maximum of size and color in the hills and valleys of lower New England. Come to a roadside there that is splashed with purple and gold and you have come upon a stand of New England asters at their September best.

There are dozens of native asters, but the big purple one is queen of them all, both in size and color. Others range from tiny whites through medium-sized lavenders, and all are lavish in their offering of bloom. But the New England aster is often two inches across, rich with royal color, and sometimes stands six feet tall. Perhaps the blossom center is no more golden than that of any other aster, but the deep purple of the surrounding rays makes it look like a twenty-four-karat coin.

It is so beautiful that gardeners sometimes grow it. It appreciates such care but never demands it. With root room at any roadside, it asks no favors. Even the crews that neaten the roadsides seldom discourage it; a midsummer mowing may shorten its steps, but September finds it eye-catching, spectacular. I sometimes think it was for this that the whole aster tribe evolved. If there is royalty among the wildflowers, the New England aster certainly is a member.

Common Mullein

I like this big mullein as much for its leaves as for its small yellow flowers, with which it is so parsimonious. I go out into my pastures any wintry day when the snow has melted or been blown away along an old stone wall, and there I find several big rosettes of gray-green mullein leaves. The outer ones, which look almost like the leaves of a tobacco plant except that they are light green and very fuzzy, are rather worn and withered by January, and they are beaten down flat on the ground by the snow. But the inner leaves of the rosette are vaguely green with the promise of April.

Then when spring comes, those inner leaves liven up and the tall stalk begins to grow. Producing that stalk is the plant's purpose, for on its tip will be the flowers and, after them, the seeds. The stalk grows five, six, sometimes eight feet tall, slender as a ship's mast, sturdy as an oak. It has green, woolly leaves that hug the stem at intervals, and by June it has a head of buds, a fat thumb of them at the very tip. Eventually those buds open into small, rather bright-yellow flowers, five-petaled and with no noticeable odor. Only a few flowers open at the same time, half a dozen at most. The plant is a biennial and dies after the second year.

The name *mullein* is said to be a corruption of the Latin word *mulandrum*, from which comes *melanders*, meaning leprosy. At one time, mullein was believed to be a cure for leprosy. It has been used a long time in herbal medicine, as a mild narcotic, as a sedative, and as a relief from asthma—the asthmatic person smokes the dried leaves. The plant has a score of common names, among them velvet leaf, velvet dock, torches, blanket leaf, cow's lungwort, velvet plant, Adam's flannel, and old man's flannel.

Bouncing Bet

SAPONARIA OFFICINALIS

If bouncing Bet were not so common and so generous with its blossoms, it probably would be a treasured plant for the flower garden. But it grows at every roadside, and it blooms from June until hard frost. It welcomes the daisies, and it is still here to bid good-bye to the goldenrod. It is like drifted snow at the country roadside, and sometimes its drifts are tinged with pink. As plants, the Bets belong to the pink family, and they have that welcome old-time spicy pink fragrance. In color they range from pure white to a delicate magenta-pink, the color appearing in the petals' veining.

This species was brought to America from Europe, both as a garden flower and as a household convenience. Another common name is soapwort, and its botanical name indicates that it is saponific. Long ago its roots were used as a soap, particularly for washing women's hair but also for delicate underclothing. In the South it once was called my lady's wash bowl.

I have often wondered who was the Bet for which it was named. Or was Bet one of those more or less generic names, for milkmaids, perhaps, or for barmaids? And did those particular Bets bounce as they walked? Probably. In any case, here is Bet immortalized, whoever she was; and it couldn't be in a more comfortable, everyday, sweet-smelling flower. We should all be glad that the plants brought here from Europe and grown in the herb gardens did leap the wall or creep through the fence and take to the fields.

Caryophyllaceae

Queen Anne's Lace

DAUCUS CAROTA

It's the wild carrot that frills the fencerows with white, lacy heads in midsummer, and its fine-cut bright green foliage is almost the color of that of the tame carrots in the garden. The root, however, is very different—tough, bitter, and not at all tasty. The name *Queen Anne's lace* pays tribute to the flat-topped heads of florets, dainty as fine lace and pretty enough to deck a queen. Some call it bird's nest, because as the flower heads ripen into seeds the stems curl upward and form a cup-shaped basket much like a bird's nest.

In the center of most wild carrot flowers one finds a single purple floret, the jewel or amethyst as it is often called. Some casual observers use this purple floret as their means of differentiating between the wild carrot and the somewhat similar flower head of the yarrow; but it is an unreliable index, for some wild carrots have no jewel. Actually, the yarrow heads are loose and the bloom has a grayish tinge, while the wild carrot is clear white. Besides, the foliage of the two plants is quite different.

The wild carrot may be a roadside weed, but it carries a royal name. Which Anne it was named for remains a puzzle. Anne of Brittany was Queen of France, Anne of Denmark became the wife of James I of England, Anne of Austria became the wife of France's Louis XIII, and James II's daughter Anne married Prince George of Denmark and became Britain's queen. All wore lace, of course, the finest lace of their time, and to have been named for any of them would have been high tribute. But a queen's lace now decorates the roadside, and the queen herself is forgotten. "Vanity of vanities . . . all is vanity."

Wild Cucumber

ECHINOCYSTIS LOBATA

This roadside vine with the eye-catching clusters of small white flowers in June belongs to the same family as the cucumbers we eat as dill pickles. Botanically the family is Cucurbitaceae and it also includes gourds, squashes, and melons. The botanical name of this particular member of the family comes from the Greek *echinos*, for hedgehog, and *cystis*, for bladder, referring to the fat, prickly seed pods. The *lobata* means lobed and refers to the leaves, something like maple leaves but with five pointed lobes.

Wild cucumber loves damp places, such as riverbanks. It grows quickly, being an annual. It climbs by its three-pronged tendrils, which grab and twine on anything in reach. Along my riverbank it sometimes drapes bushes so vigorously that it almost smothers them. It even climbs trees to a height of fifteen or twenty feet. But it particularly likes to climb and sprawl all over our garden fences, along with wild grapes and Virginia creeper. It more or less makes up for its pushy habit in June and July when it almost covers itself with those clusters of six-pointed little white star flowers. Those, however, are only the staminate flowers, the males. The pistillate flowers are borne in pairs, quite inconspicuous, at the base of the leaf stems. It is from those pistillate flowers that the prickly pods form. They do look like small fat cucumbers covered with rather soft green prickles. If they had more "flesh" in them, they might be edible. But they are mostly air, with a few membranes and two or three seeds inside.

These plants have good years and bad. In good years they are everywhere. In bad years there are only a few of them.

Celandine

CHELIDONIUM MAJUS

This roadside plant, usually considered a weed, is sometimes called swallowwort, and its botanical name comes from the Greek word for swallow, the bird. Back in the days of early Greek plant study it was said that mother swallows gathered the yellowish juice from this plant to wash out the eyes of their nestlings and give them good eyesight. Hence the name.

Celandine really belongs to the poppy family. The presence of the yellowish juice in the stems is evidence of that. The small, four-petaled yellow flowers, which open wide and give not even the slightest hint of the familiar tulip cup, bloom by late April or early May. The plants have bright green leaves that appear in mid-March or early April, one of the earliest roadside signs of vernal awakening. In England it is virtually evergreen, particularly when allowed to grow beside an old wall.

According to *Gerard*'s *Herball*, "The juice of Celandine is good to sharpen the sight, for it cleanseth and consumeth away slimie things that cleave about the ball of the eye and hinder the sight, and especially being boiled with hony in a brazen vessell." It was also believed that the root, if chewed, was a cure for toothache. And for falconers with sick or ailing hawks, it was said, "The root cut into small pieces is good to be given to Hauks against sundry diseases, whereunto they are subject."

Teasel

DIPSACUS SYLVESTRIS

You seldom hear about teasel flowers, which are small, lavender, and bloom in a tight cluster at the tips of the stems. The cluster is egg-shaped and almost the size of a small hen's egg. When the blossoms fade, they leave this egg-shaped cluster of seed pods, each with a long, slender bract, or thorn, often slightly hooked at the end. It makes me think of a big burdock bur, though the teasel isn't nearly as vicious as the burdock. In pioneer days and for some years thereafter, teasel heads were used to comb wool for spinning and to raise the nap on newly woven cloth. Some say they were used for "fulling" cloth, but that is wrong. A slightly variant species, *Dipsacus fullonum*, perpetuates the error in its name.

The teasels were originally brought here from Europe to provide those thorny pods for the weavers. The plants throve in the New England soil and went wild. The *sylvestris* in the botanical name simply means "of the woods." Teasel prefers damp woodland margins. A few years ago I found a patch of teasel growing at the edge of a small woodland bog just up the road from my own farm. They probably had been there for many years, but because their flowers were inconspicuous, I had never before noticed them.

Small maggots are often found in teasel heads. Those maggots were once believed to be a cure for ague and other afflictions if "hanged about the neck," but herbalist Gerard scoffed at this. "Notwithstanding Physicke charmes, these wormes hanged about my neck . . . and divers such foolish toies," Gerard wrote, "I say my helpe came from God himselfe, for these medicines and all other such things did me no good at all."

Winter Cress

BARBAREA VULGARIS

This mild member of the mustard family is sometimes called yellow rocket. It also, long ago, was the herb of Saint Barbara, and its seed was sown in western Europe on or near Saint Barbara's Day, December 4. We call it Barbara's cress, and we pluck it early in the spring for a green that we eat either raw in salad or cooked lightly and buttered, a special April treat. Sometimes we mix it with other early wild greens, but not often. It is a special flavor all by itself.

Most of the mustards make good greens, but some are bitter. Like certain other spring greens, some are poisonous to one degree or another unless they are cooked. Our list of salad greens from the roadside and meadow starts with this winter cress; it also includes lamb's quarters and peppergrass and one of the sorrels that grows in the borders of our vegetable garden. The list of cooked greens is much more varied, but, there too, we always include some of the mustards.

Winter cress grows in dampish places along our brooks and on the riverbank, and it grows at the edge of the woodland where it has to fight for root room. After the first few weeks it becomes tall and rank, its flower stalks sometimes two feet tall. Then it is just another weed, to be cut—not pulled, because then it would not produce those tender rosettes of tasty leaves next spring. So we keep it under control by mowing, since it isn't a pest to be rooted out.

Dame's Rocket

HESPERIS MATRONALIS

Common and botanical names are all entwined for this flower. *Hesperis* comes from the Greek for evening or evening-star. *Matronalis* comes from the Latin for matronly. It has also been known as mother-of-the-evening and dame's violet, as well as dame's rocket. And I have heard it called—or miscalled, really—wild phlox. It is no kin of the phlox. It belongs to the mustard family, as its four petals indicate; phlox has five petals. I have also heard this flower called wandering lady, and with good reason.

Dame's rocket grows in old fields and along country roads, looking something like a phlox plant, up to three feet in height. Its blossoms come at the top of the stalks, in clusters similar to those of phlox. In color it varies from white through shades of pink to a deep violet, almost purple. And it is definitely a wanderer. Twenty years ago there was a small patch of it almost two miles down the road from my house. I admired it when it came to blossom but never picked it or tried to scatter its seeds. Fifteen years ago it was within a mile of my house. Five years ago it was within half a mile. Two years ago it appeared on the riverbank in front of our house.

Dame's rocket was brought to America from Europe as a garden flower and escaped to the open fields. Its seeds do have the sharp-tanged bite of all members of the mustard family and could be used as a condiment. If there is any doubt about the plant's identity, watch for the seedling. If it is rocket, it forms long, slender seed pods that stand upright on the stems. The flower, by the way, is quite fragrant, unlike most of the mustards.

The Old Pasture

The old pasture has become a familiar feature of many summer homes in New England. Urban people buy a farm, renovate and modernize the house, but they neither farm the fields nor graze the pastures, which they think of as open spaces, natural grasslands, beautiful vistas. They forget that the farmer plowed those fields and mowed those pastures. Left to themselves for five years, they become tangles of brush and briars. In ten years they are young woodlands, with birch and ash and cedar seedlings ten feet high and fighting for sun and root room. But for those few transition years, the old field and the old pasture are perfect places to look for wildflowers.

There are two such pastures within half an hour's walk from our house. Both are edged with wild fencerows along the road, natural growth of scrub trees and bushes that are the homes, hiding places, and pantries of birds and small animals. From there the old pasture I most often visit spreads across a gentle slope to the hillside, follows the hill to an old ledge now crumbled into gravelly soil, and at the top is bordered by a thin woodland.

Find such a place, start at the road, and you can spend an afternoon in the fencerow. Depending on the season, it will have anything from bloodroot and Jack-in-the-pulpit to asters and goldenrod, from wild strawberries to highbush cranberries. It may even have in one of its hidden openings a small stand of fringed gentians. If you find them, keep the secret. Talk of buttercups, of fleabane, of wild geraniums. In one such fencerow I recently found goatsbeard, a tall plant with a compound flower spike of tiny white blossoms. It is related to hardhack and meadowsweet. I hadn't seen it anywhere in ten years.

Start across the foot of this old pasture, and watch your feet. You will be walking on bluets, which come to flower, like a carpet of hoarfrost, in late April. Or on wild phlox or wild strawberries. In the tufts of grass you will see blue-eyed grass and Deptford pinks. There will be buttercups everywhere. As the summer comes toward August there will be hawkweed in patches that are so colorful they don't seem natural; they must have been painted. Chicory will be there, in bright blue blossoms on sunny days. Look for the chicory in a dry corner with poor soil.

Go up the hillside toward the old ledge and the gravelly soil, and if it is spring watch for the little white anemones, the lavender or pink or white hepaticas, the saxifrage. And the columbines. I think of the first week in May and the crimson-and-gold columbines in the same instant; and I always find the columbines on those rocky slopes. Elsewhere too, but always there.

On up to the edge of the woods, where there is leaf mold and partial shade, and there you will find the wild ginger, the showy orchis, the May apple, the bloodroot; sometimes, if you have lived right and said the proper prayers, you will find trailing arbutus.

And there you are, at the top of the hill, the whole of that old pasture dropping away down to the road in the valley. A perfect site for a house with a view—if you didn't have to get up that hill on an icy January day. And if that handsome old pasture wasn't going to become a tangle of brush and briars in a few years, a scraggly woodland eventually. Forget that house. Let the old pasture be as it is. Let it become what it will. You have seen it, with all its wildflowers, all its natural celebration of life. You will own it, in memory, for as long as you care to remember.

Blue-Eyed Grass

SISYRINCHIUM ANGUSTIFOLIUM

That is a very big botanical name for a very small flower, and it really doesn't mean anything special. The *Sisyrinchium* is a Greek name used for some other plant by Theophrastus, back in the third century B.C., and much, much later picked up and transferred to the present species. The *angustifolium* simply means narrow-leafed. The common name, blue-eyed grass, suits it very well.

It belongs to the iris family, though you would never know it by the flower. It is shaped like a Deptford pink blossom, except the pink has five petals, the blue-eyed grass six. And blue-eyed grass petals all end in a thorn-shaped point that I doubt has ever pricked even the softest finger. The individual flowers are a deep blue, a clear, clean blue, and they are seldom as much as half an inch across. In the center of each little flower is a six-pointed star-shaped white marking with bright golden yellow accents. Each point of the star extends out into a petal.

But the flowers are so small that such details are usually over-looked unless one stops and examines them. The flowers are born individually, but two or three may appear at or near the tip of each tall, slim green leaf. The flowers mature into small round seed capsules on hairlike stems. The whole plant stands only about a foot high, though it may grow taller when in the midst of tall grass trying to reach the sun.

These little perennials are surprising spangles in the damp meadows in May and can sometimes be found blooming there as late as July.

most in
may - July

1' high

6 petals

Wood Lily

LILIUM PHILADELPHICUM

There are half a dozen large lilies, all some shade of yellow, orange, or red, that grow wild in my area. At least three of them are "escapes," species originally cultivated; but two, the wood lily and the field or meadow lily, are definitely wild. The wood lily is one of the most beautiful of all. It is easily recognizable because its flowers stand upright, and the petals narrow to the dimension of stems, making the typical lily cup open at the base. All the other field lilies have closed cups and hang downward from their stems.

The wood lily's leaves grow in fives, arranged in whorls, one above another on central stalks three to five feet tall. The stalks branch at the top into two or three stems on which the flowers are borne.

The meadow lily is a taller, more slender plant and may have as many as twenty flowers at the tip of its stalk. These flowers are closed cups with recurving petals, and all hang face-downward. The Turk's cap lily also has flowers that face downward, but its petals recurve more than the meadow lily's. And they are more liberally spotted with purplish dots.

All these flowers are often called tiger lilies, because of their spots, though tigers are striped not spotted.

In medieval times, lily bulbs were crushed and mixed with honey as a cure for ulcers and scurvy. American Indians ate them roasted. They are nutritious, taste like a sweetish potato. Today they are protected by law in many states.

Yellow Meadow Lily

L I L I U M   C A N A D E N S E

This lily is sometimes called a Turk's cap and sometimes plain Canada lily. It really isn't the Turk's cap, *Lilium superbum,* which grows much taller, as much as seven feet, and has leaves on the upper part of the stem set alternately instead of in whorls. And the petals of the Turk's cap curl far back, almost touching each other.

This Canada lily, however, is a beautiful flower with true lily trumpets which nod so that the flowers face the ground. Their color is a buff-yellow on the outside and an orange-buff on the inside, with a liberal specking of purple spots on the inside. It has plenty of nectar, which is protected from the rain by the position of the pendulous blossom. Wild bees gather that nectar, and they also gather the brown pollen from the flower's long stamens.

I find both the yellow meadow lily and the wood lily in my pastures, most often along one of the brooks or in a dampish place watered by a brook. They don't like bogs, but they do prefer lowlands to dry uplands. I also occasionally find them at the edge of a woodland. But for some reason they don't seem to "stay put" on my place. I find them in one spot for two or three years, but then they disappear, only to appear somewhere else. They do grow from seed, of course, but I am not sure how that seed is distributed.

Montiaceae

Spring Beauty

CLAYTONIA VIRGINICA

I first knew spring beauties in southeastern Pennsylvania, where they were always among the first of all spring flowers. You could look across a meadow one day and see nothing but greening grass, and the next afternoon that same meadow would be dappled with pink and white—the spring beauties had come to flower. It was beautiful. Later I learned that when I, as a small boy, was searching the damp woods of Nebraska for dogtooth violets for May baskets, youngsters in the East were picking spring beauties for their May baskets. They do bloom early, as early as March in specially favored places, such as a south slope with a grove of woodland above it to fend off the cold winds.

Individually, the spring beauties are of no particular importance. They are small white or pink flowers little more than half an inch across, veined with a deeper pink but with a warm yellow heart and golden stamens. The flowers are at the tips of the stems, seldom more than nine inches or a foot tall. The early bees love them and cross-pollinate them. They have linear grasslike leaves, which clasp the stem.

Andrew Wyeth painted a particularly handsome picture of a clump of spring beauties and called it *Quaker Ladies*, after another common name of the flower. Some also know the flower as patience, though I have no idea why.

Deptford Pink

DIANTHUS ARMERIA

These tiny pinks, looking like miniature sweet William flowers, are usually called crimson in color, though to my eye they are deeper than crimson, nearer to maroon. They grow in my pastures, sometimes reaching up eighteen inches for the sunlight, and their color catches my eye every time I walk there from early June till mid-September. Looking at them closely, you see that the petals are fringed and sparsely dotted with white. The buds form in clusters at the tip of the stem and open one or two at a time. The leaves are long and narrow, grasslike. The flowers, less than half an inch across, have five petals and are fertilized by bees and butterflies.

The Deptford pink was brought here by early English colonists as a garden flower, escaped and went wild. Now you will find it in fields and along roadsides from Maine through Maryland and west beyond Michigan. The Deptford in its name comes from an old administrative division of London, now part of Lewisham. Deptford had its own colorful history. In Elizabethan times it was a noted cattle market and site of the royal dockyards. It also had taverns patronized by playwrights, poets, and, some said, disreputable characters. Christopher Marlowe was murdered there in a brawl because, according to one story, he was a government agent spying on certain criminals.

The name *pink*, a botanical family name, may be short for pink eye and comes from the Dutch *pinck oog*, meaning a small eye. If so, it would seem that the color pink was named for the flowers, not vice versa. *Dianthus* is from the Greek *dios*, the god Zeus, and *anthos*, flower. In other words, a divine flower.

84

Common Buttercup

RANUNCULUS ACRIS

This is the buttercup of the meadow, the one that small children visiting the country often pluck by the handful, only to find that it withers before they can get it home and into a vase of water. It thrives in meadows, in pastures, and at roadsides at least in part because of its bitter taste—that is what that *acris* in the botanical name means, acrid. Few animals eat it.

Buttercup yellow is one of the clearest of all flower colors, a brilliant golden yellow. Buttercups are perennials and come up early in the spring. I have seen them appear in March and, like a number of other early plants, they are able to "run a fever" and literally melt their way up through the last inch or so of snow. By late May they are everywhere.

The old herbals warned that buttercups were to be used sparingly and with caution in preparation of simples. They are mildly poisonous unless cooked, and not very palatable then. However, the early settlers esteemed buttercups for making pickles. They took the buds, just before they opened, and steeped them in vinegar.

The Indians boiled the roots and ate them. (Boiling took care of that poisonous tinge.) They gathered the seeds, parched them, and made meal, which they baked into cakes. They also used the plant's juice for a yellow dye.

Tall Meadow-Rue

THALICTRUM POLYGAMUM

In early April I have, on occasion, mistaken the first leaves and shoots of tall meadow-rue for wild columbine thrusting up through the litter and leaf mold at the edge of the woods. The leaves are much the same shape, and both are a light bluish-green shade at that time. But from that point on, there is no resemblance. The meadow-rue shoots up rapidly, three, four, sometimes six feet tall, openly branched, and the tiny white flowers bloom in foamy clusters at the tips of the branching stems. The meadow-rues are handsome plants, and they grow in damp meadows from Maine south and west to Illinois. However, I have also found these flowers thriving in pockets of leaf mold on rocky ledges high above a lake.

This flower really has no kinship to the classic rue, one of the bitter herbs long used in medicine, probably to strengthen that dark brown taste. It is a member of the crowfoot family, and a second cousin of the columbine for which I mistake it now and then. How it got the name *rue* is a mystery nobody seems to have thought worth unraveling. The *Thalictrum* in its botanical name comes from the Greek name for a plant mentioned but never identified by Dioscorides. A mystery, wrapped in an enigma.

The Indians gathered and dried the leaves of rue, crushed them and rolled them into a cigarette, then blew the smoke into the ears of a deaf person. It was said to be a sure cure.

Chinese Mustard

BRASSICA JUNCEA

Few weeds are more disliked by the farmer than the alien mustards. That is one reason they have so many common names: wild mustard, field kale, curlock, bastard rocket, runch weed, kraut weed, field curse, charlock, kedlock. The botanical name literally means "field cabbage."

One reason mustards are so disliked is that they are among the most persistent of all field weeds, and grow almost everywhere in the northern part of the United States. Mustard flourishes in new fields. It persists in old fields. Tests made by the U.S. Department of Agriculture have shown that a mustard seed will sprout and grow even after being buried for forty years. So once it gets a start in a field and goes to seed there, it will appear every time that field is plowed and seed is brought to the surface.

It is in the ground in my pastures and meadows, though we seldom see a plant unless we plow that field to renew the grass. Then here comes the mustard, always. And I go out, when it is coming to blossom and is easily spotted, and pull it, every plant I can find. That puts an end to the mustard in that field until it is plowed again.

Wild mustard does have a rather pretty yellow four-petaled flower about half an inch across. It blooms in clusters at the tip of the stems and matures seed pods that are long and slim, packed with little black seeds. Pioneers ground these seeds and used them for a condiment. Indians and pioneers made a paste of the ground seed for plasters to treat chest colds. We gather mustard leaves while they are still young for a mess or two of cooked greens every spring.

Wild Geranium

GERANIUM MACULATUM

The wild geranium is also often called cranesbill because its seed pods are shaped like the long, pointed beak of a crane. The flower is a five-petaled, magenta-pink or lavender-purple blossom and is borne in clusters at the tip of the stalk. The plant grows as much as two feet tall in thin woodlands and at the side of rural roads. It is relatively common over the eastern half of the United States.

A cousin of the domestic geranium, it blooms from mid-May through July and even longer in many places. It has a smaller wild cousin called herb Robert that blooms till hard frost. Both plants have the typical geranium odor and attract Japanese beetles. In the early years of the battle with Japanese beetles, an essence of that fragrance named geraniol was used as bait in beetle traps.

The wild geranium was used in early medicine by both whites and Indians. The root contains a strong astringent. A tea made from it was used for diarrhea, hemorrhages, ulcers, and wounds. The fibers of the root were used in poultices and dressings for running sores and wounds. Drunk as a tea, wild geranium was one of the most widely used means of birth control among the Indians. It was supposed to keep the user from becoming pregnant for a year, if properly used.

If you have an hour to spare, go looking for "blue-eyed" wild geraniums. Some of the blossoms, but by no means all or even all those on the same plant, have beautiful peacock-blue anthers. The anthers are the pollen-bearing tips of the stamens.

The name, both common and botanical, comes from the old Greek word *geranos*, meaning a crane.

Cow Parsnip

HERACLEUM LANTANUM

The wild parsnips all belong to the parsley family and are cousins of Queen Anne's lace. The roots of none of them, however, are good to eat, and they are virulently poisonous. One of them is the so-called hemlock, a brew of which was used by the ancient Greeks to execute prisoners. That is the hemlock Socrates is said to have been forced to drink.

Cow parsnip is one of the nonpoisonous species. The Indians ate the young, tender leaves and stalks as spring greens, using them either raw or cooked. They made poultices for various maladies out of the crushed roots. A tea made from the flowers was supposed to be good for headaches. The dried and powdered root was added to hot baths to cure paralysis of the legs. For rheumatism both the Indians and the Spanish people of the Southwest drank a brew of cow parsnip roots. And a poultice of the mashed roots was believed to draw out the poison of a rattlesnake bite.

The plant grows in neglected fields and other wasteland over much of the United States. It is a tall perennial that comes up fresh year after year, sends up a stout, hollow, ridged central stem, sometimes six or eight feet tall, and comes to blossom with flat clusters of small, dull white flowers, each with five notched petals. The leaves are compound, in three divisions, toothed and deeply lobed, and there is a broad swelling at the junction of leaf stem and plant stem. The seeds are broad, flat, and oval. The botanical name comes from Hercules, who thought the plant had unusually important medicinal qualities. Maybe his ghost told the Indians.

Butterfly Weed

ASCLEPIAS TUBEROSA

This is the showiest of all the milkweeds, with brilliant orange blossoms. It blooms in clusters, like other milkweeds, but here the clusters are erect, at the top of the stems, and flat-topped. You can see one of these plants almost a quarter of a mile away, it is so bright. And you can see the butterflies even if the plant is hidden behind a bush. It attracts all kinds of butterflies, including the monarchs, the familiar milkweed butterflies.

— lung inflammation

Another common name for the plant is pleurisy root, which points to one use the old herbalists made of it. The root was boiled and a decoction made which was thought to ease the pains of pleurisy. Whether this particular milkweed's root was better than that of the common milkweed, I have no idea. The Indians used this, as they did the other milkweeds, as an emetic, a cathartic, and an expectorant. And, perhaps because its juice was milky, it was used by the Indians to treat a nursing mother's sore breasts and to improve lactation.

I have seen this butterfly weed grown in gardens. Then, of course, it was called butterfly milkweed. It does make a handsome garden flower, and it thrives under cultivation. I happen to prefer it in the wild, and I know a rocky cliff on the shore of a small lake where there are half a dozen plants that have been there for years. They persist because nobody can climb up or down that cliff to pick the flowers or dig up the plants. I want to cheer every time I see them in bloom.

96

Black-Eyed Susan

R U D B E C K I A   H I R T A

Black-eyed Susan's eyes aren't really black at all. They are a purplish-brown, as anyone who takes more than a passing glance at the Susans that brighten July's roadsides and meadows can see. The Susan is a biennial that came from west of the Mississippi River, where, mixed with clover, it was native to the prairies many years ago. Once in the East it took to the soil and climate with vigor and pertinacity. Now its dark-eyed, orange-petaled flowers are common from Maine southward, wherever it finds a foothold. And it is adaptable to almost any foothold available.

The petals have a peculiarly rich golden-orange color. They are full of sunlight. Like so many of the Compositae, its petals vary in number, thirteen on this flower, fifteen on another of the same plant, fourteen on still a third. And they curl and twist, sometimes fraying out at the tips for no obvious reason. The flower's sepals, the green "petals" that encase the bud and later form a background for the flower, outnumber the petals, sometimes by as much as two to one. And there are countless florets encircling the disk, Susan's eye. They open tiny blossoms in succession and ring the disk with still another halo of golden-orange, the ripened pollen.

Bees and butterflies love the Susans, and so do most country youngsters. Weeds they certainly are when they invade the garden, but at the roadside they are bright and jaunty and full of the summer sun. And they don't discourage easily, as many a gardener knows. Cut them or pull them up—they'll be back, as surely as the July sunshine, to which they belong.

Ox-Eye Daisy

CHRYSANTHEMUM LEUCANTHEMUM

Summer wouldn't be summer without daisies, even though the common field daisy known to almost every man, woman, and child is sometimes called farmer's curse. Any farmer can tell you why. Daisies populate roadsides, but they invade pastures, meadows, and all kinds of cultivated fields, and the invasion is en masse. So while most farmers smile at picnicking youngsters who gather fistfuls of daisies, they frown in utter bafflement at summer visitors who actually pick daisies and arrange them in vases.

The daisy is kin to the chrysanthemum, as its botanical name shows, and is a member of the big and varied composite family. The flower's golden center consists of a mass of botanically perfect miniature blossoms, each complete with stamens and a pistil. The white petals actually are rays, each the single petal of a miniature pistillate flower. When the petals wither and the flower head ripens, it produces a whole packet of seeds. These seeds have vigorous vitality; hence the persistence of the daisy.

The daisy's name comes from "day's eye" and refers to the yellow center, which folklore represented as the sun. Sometimes the common field daisy is called the ox-eye daisy, for which there is little reason since most oxen's eyes are brown, not yellow. But the name *daisy* is loosely applied to black-eyed Susans, and even to asters, so the name doesn't much matter, really. Daisies grow in vacant lots and even in the city's concrete gutters, if they can find a crack. And to the unbiased eye they are beautiful, even in a meadow. Unless you happen to be a farmer.

Pasture Thistle

CIRSIUM PUMILUM

There are about a dozen species of these thistles, all called *Cirsium* by the botanists, a name given to them by Dioscorides, the old Greek physician and herbalist, because he used them to reduce swollen veins, and the Greek word for a swollen vein is *cirsos*. Thus do botanical names have their origins.

This is the largest-flowered of all the common thistles. Its solitary heads, light purplish-lavender in color, may be as much as two or even three inches across. And they are very fragrant and rich in nectar. Bumblebees love them and perch on them, sipping the nectar till they are too intoxicated to fly away. Their leaves are light green in color and very prickly, though the prickles are shorter than those on the leaves of the Canada thistle, for instance. And pasture thistles seldom grow more than thirty inches high. Some other species grow five and six feet high. When the flower heads ripen, the floss is gleaming white, and goldfinches love to tear them apart to get at the seeds, which are small and dark.

White settlers disliked the thistles, which were a nuisance in the fields and a pain in the pants, if one sat on them. But the Indians had many uses for them. They peeled the stalk, boiled it, and ate it. They made a decoction from the roots for diarrhea. They used the juice from mashed, boiled roots to treat earache, and they held this juice, hot, in the mouth for toothache. It seems to have been an all-purpose tea, because they also used it to hasten and ease childbirth.

Asteraceae

Chicory

CICHORIUM INTYBUS

Like a good many other wildlings, chicory is too abundant for the good of its own reputation. If it were a rarer plant, the beauty of its blossoms and the clean, clear quality of their blue would more often be noted and admired. For the chicory blossom is an example of one of the best blues in the floral spectrum, blue as the innocent eyes of a six-year-old blonde. Only the flowers of the flax plant can compete with it in color.

But chicory grows along the dry and gravelly roadsides, ubiquitous as ragweed. It grows where little else can find a roothold, and it persists in heat and drought. Come mid-July and it rears its slim stalks and opens its flowers, like a baby-blue mist; and if the season is particularly dry, it seems to thrive as few other plants do, thrive and bloom in profusion. Not even the yellow evening primroses, which also make the best of waste places, can make so much of so little encouragement.

One reason for chicory's colorful presence is the long, vigorous root from which it springs. And that root is the reason chicory was first brought to America from its native Europe. For generations, Europeans have harvested the chicory root, dried and roasted it and used it as a substitute and adulterant for coffee. Early Americans used chicory in the same way and grew their own supply. They also used its young leaves for salad. Thus it got its foothold here, escaping from fields and gardens. Now it is a weed and in poorly tended fields it can be a nuisance. But it also lends a touch of roadside beauty, a handsome flower whose chief offense is being so common and so persistent.

King-Devil

HIERACIUM PRATENSE

There are almost a score of species of hawkweeds listed in the big botanical manuals, but they all divide into two groups, the yellow, represented by the king-devil, and the orange, of which the tawny hawkweed is typical. The yellows nearly always are smooth-stemmed, the oranges covered with dark hairs like a one-day growth of beard on a dark-complexioned man's face. Another common name for the orange species is devil's paintbrush.

The botanical name for hawkweeds, *Hieracium*, comes from the Greek, *hierax*, meaning a hawk. The old Greeks believed, and it was written by Pliny, that hawks used the juice of this plant to strengthen their eyesight. One version of the story is that they suck the juice and carry it to their nests to bathe the eyes of their nestlings.

King-devil is a beautiful bright yellow, almost a dandelion yellow. The orange species is a deep red-orange, one of those colors you can see a quarter of a mile away. The plants have become field weeds, seem to have no particular use except as pretty flowers, and are not poisonous to man or beast, so far as I can learn. A few years ago on a midsummer trip to Maine, I saw hawkweed of both orange and yellow species practically smothering hayfields. It was beautiful to look at, but it must have been a major pest to the farmers. It grows here in my own pastures, but on no such scale as that. Nowhere in my own area is it so widespread that it has become a problem.

Cardinal Flower

LOBELIA CARDINALIS

One of the most pleasant surprises I have when I prowl the lower mountainside in September is when I find the cardinal flowers. They are such a beautiful cardinal red, and they are so full of color that it tinges the stem and upper leaves. September isn't a red flower month—the reds are midsummer colors; and that makes the cardinal flower even more spectacular.

The cardinal flower is a lobelia. The botanical name simply honors one Matthias de l'Obel, a seventeenth-century Flemish herbalist. Most of the lobelias are some shade of blue, like the great lobelia which blooms only a little earlier than the cardinal flower. Its flower has a long tube that divides into three long petal-like lips. There is nectar at the bottom of that long tube, but few insects can reach it. Only hummingbirds, with their long beaks, can get to it; and by the time the cardinal flower blooms, many of the hummers have gone south. So there is little cross-fertilization, little seeding. Mostly the plant multiplies by perennial offshoots. That is why you usually will find several plants, or even a whole cluster of them, where you find one. And they will be there year after year if they are not dug up or otherwise pillaged.

There is a minor cousin called Indian tobacco, *Lobelia inflata*, which grows almost everywhere and blooms from July to October. It grows as a single stem seldom over two feet tall, with oval leaves and fat little seed pods following the tiny light blue flowers. The dried leaves can be smoked like tobacco, but they taste like weeds.

108

Common Tansy

TANACETUM VULGARE

Walking along a country roadside or across an old field, you may smell tansy before you notice its blossoms. The plant's foliage is strongly, sharply aromatic. Its flowers look something like daisies that have lost all their petals—tansy flowers consist only of that central disk, the "eye" composed of a compact cluster of florets. The plant is a common roadside weed from Maine to the Carolinas and west to the Rockies.

Long ago, in England they gave the name *tansy* to the plant we know as yarrow, and in many places in this country the names seem to be interchangeable. So the old records can be quite confusing. It is true, however, that the two plants, while quite different botanically, do have many of the same herbal qualities. And it was for these qualities that tansy was valued in fifteenth- and sixteenth-century England and among America's Indians and early white settlers.

The Indians used both tansy and yarrow to brew a tea. They made a decoction of leaves and stems, which had the usual "tonic" properties. They made poultices from the roots to apply to wounds and swellings. From the whole tansy plant they brewed a drink that was used for "a weak or disordered stomach" and for "cramp in the womb during menstruation." The Indians dried the blossoms, powdered them, and administered them to expel intestinal worms.

In England it was said that tansy tea was a good beverage "for the poor," though it is uncertain whether the recommendation was for reasons of health or economy.

Asteraceae

Early Goldenrod

SOLIDAGO JUNCEA

I think of goldenrod as an autumn flower, but it really belongs to late summer. By August the yellow of goldenrod has begun to make roadsides and meadow margins glow. And on a sunny afternoon the bees are almost as loud as they were at the height of the clover blossom season. Goldenrod provides a late-summer harvest that adds a special tang to autumn honey. If it weren't for the goldenrod and the asters, which also are rich in nectar, the bees would be out of business by the end of August.

Most of the goldenrods are native to this country. America has more than a hundred species, all of Europe fewer than ten, Britain only one. About twenty-five species are commonly found in the northeast corner of the United States, ranging from foot-high dwarfs to eight-foot giants. Some species, such as the anise-scented sweet goldenrod, are quite fragrant. There is even a white-flowered species, sometimes called silverrod.

The botanical name, *Solidago*, means to strengthen and refers to the plant's reputed herbal qualities. Not many of us have been dosed with an infusion of goldenrod leaves and flowers, but many of our forefathers were. One can be sure that such a brew at least strengthened one's will to be well. The plants also provide a strong yellow dye that pioneers used to brighten their winter clothing. Goldenrod yellow, one realizes, seeing it in bloom, could have brightened even the dark, dour days of December.

Goldenrod does *not* cause hay fever. Its pollen is too sticky to be airborne and annoy the allergic. Ragweed is the villain.

Fleabane

ERIGERON ANNUUS

This is commonly called daisy fleabane, in part because it looks something like a daisy. Or, since it blooms rather late, in August, something like an aster. It is neither daisy nor aster, but a close cousin of the earlier asterlike robin's plantain, which comes to blossom in May. Both have a tinge of violet in the fringing of petals around the yellowish-green center, but the color is stronger in robin's plantain.

In old herbal medicine the two, daisy fleabane and robin's plantain, were virtually interchangeable. The dried leaves were said to repel fleas, from dog or man. But the plant was more often used, as a brew of leaves and stem, for a diuretic, a tonic, a stimulant, and an astringent. Some used it for sore throat, some for rheumatism, some to shrink hemorrhoids. One researcher said that the uses for it by the Indians were "too many to list."

In my area the plant grows along roadsides and in hayfields. Farmers don't like it in their hay, though it seems never to have been reported poisonous to livestock. The flowers are smaller than daisies, and the petals are narrower than those on most asters. The botanical name comes from Greek words meaning early and old man, which comes to something like "soon becoming old." This may refer to the gray look of the plant, or it may refer to the swiftness with which the plant goes to seed after it blooms. It wastes no time, gets those seeds ripe, assures another generation.

114

Turtlehead

J. B.

C H E L O N E   G L A B R A

The turtleheads belong to the big botanical family of Scrophularia, or figworts. So do the pentstemons, the mulleins, the foxgloves, the snapdragons. Both those family names come from old folk medicine —the Scrophularia were supposed to be a good treatment for scrofula, and when called figwort they were said to be a cure for fig warts, whatever they are. The American Indians gathered turtlehead occasionally to brew a tea that was used variously as an eyewash, a laxative, or a remedy for chest colds. The English herbalists said a sprig of it hung about a person's neck preserved him from being bewitched.

Turtlehead prefers damp soil, margins of brooks, woodland marshes, the edges of swampy areas. It grows as much as six feet tall, usually two to three feet. The leaves are three to six inches long, toothed, and lance-shaped, and they grow opposite each other on the smooth stem. The flowers are clustered at the tip of the stem and are shaped somewhat like a turtle's head with the mouth partway open. They are about an inch long, white with some shade of pink at the tips. Inside are dark, woolly stamens. At first glance, the plant may be mistaken for a gentian. Bottle gentian leaves are about the same size but are smooth-edged, not notched. Fringed gentian leaves are much smaller, and also smooth-edged.

The botanical name, *Chelone*, is straight out of the Greek for turtle, indicating that the common name was used in Linnaeus's day. The *glabra* simply means smooth and refers to the absence of hairs or fuzz on the leaves and stem.

Bluets

H O U S T O N I A   C A E R U L E A

Bluets come to blossom in upland pastures and along backcountry roads in patches that look like frost on the fresh green grass of early morning. They look frosty despite their common name, for bluets are not blue at all; they are white with a tinge of lilac at the edge of the petals, and their centers are golden-yellow. They are tiny four-petaled flowers, seldom more than half an inch across, and they grow on slender stems about six inches long. In some places they are known as Quaker ladies; elsewhere they are called innocence. They grow from Maine to Georgia and west into Michigan.

Botanically, bluets belong to a strangely varied family, the madders. That family includes the coffee tree; the cinchona, from which we obtain quinine; the madder itself, from which a red dye is extracted; and the partridgeberry, that modest creeper of our eastern woods. The family also includes those sprawling, prickly, inconspicuously flowered weeds called bedstraw and goose grass.

Bluets are the smallest of the madders. One bluet in bloom is of no consequence at all. But bluets grow in patches, and in the mass they are unmistakable and demand the eye. Violets, the low, short-stemmed meadow violets, often grow with them, but they have to be searched out in the grass, while the bluets make a display. They are helped, of course, by the small butterflies which cross-fertilize them; and on a clear, sunny day the grass will be white with bluets and the air will be gay with fritillaries, clouded sulphurs, and painted ladies—May at its best.

→ Rubiaceae

@ Steptletoy

Early Saxifrage

SAXIFRAGA VIRGINIENSIS

When you are out looking for spring flowers in April, you usually can find saxifrage, in bud if not in bloom. You can spot it by finding those grayish-green rosettes of leaves, which almost hug the ground, on a rocky hillside. In the center of this leaf rosette you will find a cluster of little, fine-haired balls, no more than an eighth of an inch in diameter, and rather silvery-white in color. Those are the buds. Watch them for a couple of weeks and you will see how they shoot up on hairy stems that have no leaves, branch at the top, and open into clusters of very small, white, five-petaled flowers with golden-yellow stamens.

They are pretty little things, but quite inconspicuous even in April. Saxifrage is not an attention-grabber. The leaves are three to four inches long and lie on or close to the ground. The flower stems are six to eight inches tall, sometimes but not often as much as a foot. And they prefer dry, stony hillsides, the places where one often finds wild columbines.

There are a dozen or more species of saxifrage, most of them with only minor differences from each other. One species, however, called swamp saxifrage, prefers wet footing and in one variation has purple petals on its blossoms. The others are white or greenish-white or yellow. They form little two-beaked seed-vessels that often are madder-brown. The flowers are pollinated by early bees and probably by early butterflies such as the tortoiseshell.

The name comes from the Latin *Saxum*, a stone, and *frangere*, to break. The plant's bulblets were supposed to dissolve kidney stones. American Indians, without knowing Latin, used a saxifrage infusion as a diuretic and treatment for kidney stones.

Columbine

AQUILEGIA CANADENSIS

The columbine's common name comes from the Latin name for dove, *columba*, and reminds us that country folk long ago thought the flower's spurs looked like five tiny red doves perched in a huddle of golden sepals. Botanists call it *Aquilegia*, perhaps seeing a resemblance to the eagle's beak in those spurs, though some say that name comes from Latin *aqua*, for water, and *legere*, to collect, referring to the fluid that collects in the spurs. Some people even call these flowers meetinghouses, perhaps because the spurred petals look like a gathering of people. And some call them honeysuckles because the spurs have honey-sweet nectar in them.

The wild columbine of the East is deep red and yellow, with long, pouchy spurs, and the flowers hang on slender stems from the top of the plant. Occasionally I find one with lavender petals and whitish spurs, an unusual but not really rare variation. In the West, the Rocky Mountain columbines are bright sky-blue and white, with bigger petals and long, slim spurs. Those blue westerners are almost twice as big as the red easterners.

Among the old herbalists in England a mixture of columbine seeds and wine was used to speed and ease delivery in childbirth. The American Indians, long before Europeans came, used columbine seed alone for the same purpose. They also boiled the roots for a tea to stop diarrhea, ease coughing, and soothe an aching stomach. And they made a decoction of roots and leaves to treat biliousness and dizziness.

Hepatica

HEPATICA AMERICANA

Some call this one liverwort, some call it liverleaf, but by either name it is still hepatica, which is right out of the Greek for liver. That insidious disease, hepatitis, gets its name from the same source, the liver. The plant seems to have got its name from the shape of its leaves, lobed somewhat like a human liver.

Hepatica is one of the very earliest of all spring flowers, usually blooming in March, even in my area. I have dug into moldering leaves in January and found hepatica plants with flower buds already formed, there under the protective litter. But they wait till the deepest cold has passed and the deepest snows have melted. Then they lift those buds through the litter and open the flowers, which may be pure white, pale lavender, pale purple, or even pink. There is quite a color variation from plant to plant, but they tend to the same color in a particular spot.

New leaves usually appear at about the same time as the flowers, or soon after. The plant's old leaves persist through the winter and look rather weather-beaten until the new ones come. The flowers are from three-quarters of an inch to a full inch across and are borne on very hairy stems three or four inches long. The leaves also are woolly, particularly the new ones. The leaves are three-lobed, the lobes rounded. A closely related species called *acutiloba* has pointed leaf lobes, but its flowers are almost identical to those on *H. americana*.

Aristolochiaceae

Wild Ginger

A S A R U M   C A N A D E N S E

When apple blossoms first open on our trees, we know we can find showy orchis in bloom; and near the showy orchis will be the wild ginger, also in blossom. There always are a dozen plants of wild ginger for every showy orchis plant; but that merely proves that the orchis is rare, and the wild ginger isn't.

There is no botanical relationship between this wild ginger of our North American woodland borders and the ginger used as a spice and a condiment, which grows only in tropical and subtropical areas. But there is a gingery tang to the root of this wild ginger, which excuses the name. Maybe some pioneer cooks tried it as a seasoning or in making pickles, but I find no reference to such use as a general thing. Nor was it used in herbal medicine, according to the books I read.

You have to look twice for the flowers. The leaves are obvious. They spring up, two to a plant, on hairy stems. The leaves are heart-shaped and perhaps two and a half inches across. Beneath them, on its own stem, the flower is borne. It is purplish-brown, less than an inch across, a miniature cup that has three recurving divisions, or petals, sharp-tipped. The three sepals alternate between the petals. The flower has no particular fragrance.

The plants spread both by seed and by rhizomes, stems that travel just under the surface of the ground and send up new plants at intervals. Cut or break one of these rhizomes and you get the gingery bite in the juice exuded.

Showy Orchis

ORCHIS SPECTABILIS

Orchidaceae

The differences between orchids and orchises are botanical, and I will not even attempt to explain them. I am not sure I could. I know that some botanists say the showy orchis is the only "true orchis" in our area, and I know there are many members of the big orchid family here, from lady's-tresses, that lovely little late-summer blossom, to the big pink moccasin flowers and the other lady's-slippers. The showy orchis belongs to the family; let it go at that.

Showy orchis appears early. I find it in bloom when our apple trees come to blossom. It first appears as twin leaves, light green and five or six inches long. From between them the flower shoot appears, rises six or eight inches, and opens a cluster of small lavender and white blossoms. They are what I call orchid-shaped, with the upper petals united in a hood and beneath them the white "lip" or lower petal. The manuals sometimes call the flower's color magenta. To me it is lavender. It may vary from place to place. The showy orchises that grow on our mountainside, beside a brook and among the wild ginger, are definitely lavender, with clear white lower petals.

The name *orchid* comes from the Greek word for testicle and was given to the plants of this family because the roots of some of them were thought to resemble a man's testicles. This may be the origin of the name satyrion, by association, which was used for the family by the sixteenth-century English herbalists. Various members of the family were growing in England, but they were not used in medicine. They were simply "beautifull floures," as Gerard said.

128

Swamp Rose

ROSA PALUSTRIS

More than a hundred species of wild rose, all natives, have been described for the United States. This one, the swamp rose, is typical of the better ones, the ones I prefer, at least. It has a normal amount of thorns, grows up to seven feet high, and bears a generous number of pink blossoms. Wild roses, of course, are nearly always single flowers—that is, they have only one layer of petals. Tame roses have many leaves, a result of hybridizing.

Swamp roses bloom virtually all over the United States east of the Mississippi. They got their common name because they prefer wet places. The blossoms are often two inches across. They have the sweet fragrance typical of roses. And their flowers become big, red, rose haws, which some people gather to make into jam because they are loaded with vitamins.

The history of the rose goes far back into the mists of time. It was a favorite flower of ancient Rome. It has borne the name *rose* so long that nobody knows where it came from. It can be traced back to the Greek *rhodon*, but from there the dictionaries say vaguely, it is "of Oriental origin."

In English herbal lore, essence of rose was mixed with honey for a gargle to cure sore throats. American Indians used a rose decoction for sore eyes and for stomach and liver disorders. Rosehip tea was said to strengthen the heart. For eczema they mixed ground rose petals with wildcat fat to make a salve.

Pinxter Flower

RHODODENDRON NUDIFLORUM

Some people call this flower wild honeysuckle, though it isn't a honeysuckle at all; others call it wild azalea, which it is. It belongs to the rhododendron family. Cultivated rhododendrons are evergreens, but this pinxter flower, like almost all azaleas, is deciduous, shedding its leaves every fall. The *nudiflorum* in its botanical name means that it comes to flower while still naked, actually either just before the leaves appear or with the leaves.

That family name, *rhododendron*, comes from the Greek words for rose tree. But the "pinxter" in the common name is a puzzler. To solve it, start by altering the spelling to "pinkster," because you probably won't find the other spelling in even the unabridged dictionaries. "Pinkster" comes from the Dutch *pinksteren*, and that goes back, circuitously, to the Greek *pentekoste* which meant fifty. From there we have to go to ecclesiastical language, where we find that Pentecost, or Whitsuntide, is the fiftieth day after Easter. Whitsuntide? Oh, that meant white Sunday, when white robes were worn: it has no part in this, really. What we come out with, then, is that the pinxter is "a rose tree that blooms before it leafs out, usually seven weeks after Easter." So much for the name.

The flower is New England's own azalea, though it also grows in the South and west to Illinois. It is a shrub, seldom over six feet high, and prefers damp, cool, shady places. Its five-petaled trumpet blossoms are as much as two inches across, sweetly fragrant, and appear in various shades of pink. They bloom in clusters at the tips of the branches. The yellowish-green leaves are long, tapered at both ends.

Mountain Laurel

KALMIA LATIFOLIA

The laurel we think of when we speak of a laurel wreath, high honor among the old Greeks, was closer kin to the magnolia of today than to our mountain laurel. The American laurels are evergreens, grow from Maine to Florida, and include several species that are poisonous to animals when eaten. Hence the common names lambkill, sheepkill, etc. Mountain laurel has the most beautiful flowers of them all, white or pinkish little saucers half an inch or so across, with five lobes. They are pink in the bud, white in the prime, pink again as the flowers age. Each blossom has a small, crimson, star-shaped marking in the center. They bloom in clusters five or six inches across.

In the southern Appalachians the laurels grow in vast thickets, sometimes called slicks, and in May when they bloom they are breathtaking. In parts of New England they are equally beautiful and also once covered whole mountainsides. In a few places they still do, but such places are getting rare. In several New England states there now are laws against cutting mountain laurel or digging it up from the roadside. And quite a few communities hold annual laurel festivals.

The Indians gathered laurel leaves, dried and powdered them, and used them as a treatment of dysentery. They, and white pioneers as well, steeped the leaves and mixed them with animal fat to make an ointment for "the itch." It seems to have been effective for almost any kind of skin irritation.

The plant gets its botanical name from Peter Kalm, a German botanist and pupil of Linnaeus, who made several plant-collecting trips to the New World just before the American Revolution.

134

Purple-Flowering Raspberry

RUBUS ODORATUS

Rosaceae (handwritten)

Thimbleberry (handwritten)

The first time I saw a purple-flowering raspberry in bloom I thought the flowers were wild roses. Then I saw that the leaves were shaped like maple leaves and that the canes had no thorns. And I saw the berries, which looked like red raspberries but were almost tasteless.

This is a true raspberry, despite all these things. But the flowers are not purple. They open a strong crimson-pink and fade to magenta-pink before they wither. They are by far the biggest of all raspberry flowers, often two inches or more across. The plant itself is really a shrub, growing as much as five feet tall.

There are many raspberries, from creepers to the red-stemmed, thorny thimbleberries of my area, which make forbidding briar patches that partridges love. The purple-flowering species is also called thimbleberry, by the way. Others ripen to red berries, or to black berries, or, in some unusual instances, to white or yellow berries. All are seedy, some are sour. But the purple-flowering species is the most insipid in flavor and the most eye-catching in blossom.

Sixteenth-century England had raspberries, which *Gerard's Herball* calls "Raspis bushes" and says they grow "either with prickles upon the stalks, or else without them." It says "they groweth not wilde that I know of," and adds that "the leaves . . . boyled in water, with honey, allum and a little white wine added thereto, makes a most excellent lotion . . . and the same decoction fastneth the teeth." And eighteenth-century backwoods people in America said that raspberry-leaf tea, made as strong as possible, "will cure almost anything," even without honey or alum, but preferably well-laced with wine.

Common Cattail

TYPHA LATIFOLIA

You will find cattails almost everywhere you find bogs and wetland. They are commonly called reeds, and the dark green leaves are about an inch wide and four to ten feet tall. The flower stalk, somewhat shorter, is up to half an inch in diameter and bears the miniature flowers in a dense, cylindrical spike at the top. At the very tip is a cluster of yellowish-green male flowers that spill golden pollen down over the longer, fatter thumb of greenish-yellow female flowers just below. Then the male flowers wither, leaving a bare tip above the female flowers, which ripen into the familiar brown cattail, actually a tightly packed cylinder of fluff and minute seeds.

In the early 1900s a handful of cattails and two tail feathers from a peacock in a tall vase were considered an artistic decoration for the front parlor. Artists sneered at them, of course. But cattails have long been used by pioneers, Indians, and outdoorsmen.

Pioneers gathered and dried the leaves and wove them into rush seats for chairs. Pioneers gathered the flower stalks, still green, and boiled, buttered, and ate them like sweet corn. And pioneer women stuffed their quilts with cattail fluff, which is a good insulator. Hunters stuffed their boots and Indians stuffed their moccasins with it to ward off frostbite. Indian mothers padded cradleboards with it, both as insulation and diapers for their babies, since it is also highly absorbent. And moose, muskrats, Indians, and hungry settlers dug cattail roots and ate them. Dried or roasted, the roots could be ground into meal and then made into cakes. It has about the same food value as rice or corn.

The botanical name, *Typha*, is Greek for fen or bog.

Pickerelweed

P O N T E D E R I A   C O R D A T A

Pickerelweed is one of a whole group of what I call mud plants, which grow in sluggish streams and shallow ponds and backwaters and eventually make them into bogs: pickerelweed, mud plantain, the various arrowheads, the bur-reeds. Pickerelweed has the prettiest flowers, a whole cluster of them at the tip of the long flower stem, a flower spike four or more inches long, crowded with light blue flowers, each of which is marked with a clear yellowish-green spot.

The plant has only one leaf, dark green, thick, and shaped like a blunt arrowhead, which grows on a stem one to three feet long, just enough to raise the leaf out of the water. The flower stalk is partially sheathed at the base by the leaf's stem, and it may grow a foot taller than the leaf. The flower itself—there may be twenty or more on a spike—is funnel-shaped and divided into six petals, three of which are united above, the lower three spread apart. The flower's anthers are blue.

Nobody seems ever to have found any particular use for pickerelweed. I doubt that pickerel fish ever eat it, though they probably feed in shallow water where it grows. Muskrats sometimes eat it. Deer often do, wading into the shallow water to get it and seeming to relish it as a special treat. I have chewed pickerelweed stems and find that they have only a kind of watery, green taste. But mine is an uneducated human palate.

Skunk Cabbage

SYMPLOCARPUS FOETIDUS

Arum

Skunk cabbage probably is the earliest of all spring flowers, sometimes thrusting its purplish-streaked green and yellow hood up through the ice of a bog as early as February, almost always by March. Inside that hood is the fat spadix, a fleshy floral spike, studded with small pinkish-purple blossoms that have a rank odor, something like that of rotting meat with overtones of onion or garlic. This odor attracts carrion flies, which fertilize the blossoms. Then the big, bright green leaves, which grow to two feet or more in length, unfold. The blossoms' hood dries up, but the rank odor persists in the plant's juice—break a stem or bruise a leaf and there it is, leaving no doubt about the plant's name. To me it is a distinctly skunky odor.

Some people boast that they have boiled the leaves in several waters and eaten them for spring greens. This is possible, though it doesn't exactly perfume the house; but I would not advise any but a botanist to do it because there is another bog-loving plant with leaves enough like those of skunk cabbage to be mistaken for it, and this plant is rankly poisonous.

The Indians used skunk cabbage in their medicines, boiling the roots—which, like the roots of all arums, are fiery hot to the tongue —to make a syrup used for bronchial coughs and for asthma. They also used it as a contraceptive. One tablespoonful three times a day for three weeks was believed to insure permanent sterility in either man or woman. The raw root of the plant, pulped, was used as a poultice or liniment for rheumatism and for boils and swellings.

Few people ever see the blossoms of skunk cabbage. They smell the plant and turn away.

144

Jack-in-the-Pulpit

ARISAEMA TRIPHYLLUM

Jack-in-the-pulpit blooms early, in April, just about the time wood anemones and bloodroot appear. The flower is unique, a kind of trumpet with a long flap that curls over the top, and inside is a clublike spadix with tiny florets near its base. The arrangement is something like that of the skunk cabbage, but the Jack-in-the-pulpit does not have a rank odor. The trumpet or "pulpit" in which the "Jack" stands is sometimes all green, sometimes striped green and purplish-brown, with a great deal of variation; some botanists use this as a reason for dividing the species into several varieties. I have found that those growing in deeper shade usually have darker stripes, those in full sun lighter ones.

The Jacks prefer damp footing and thin shade, the edge of a bog-land or a damp place at the edge of a woodland. The leaves, trifold and one to a plant, are long-stemmed, sometimes two feet tall or more.

Another name for this member of the arum family is Indian turnip. But don't be fooled by that name. The root, like those of all the arum family, is fiery hot to the taste unless it is well roasted. Even roasted, it was not a staple in the Indians' diet. They did pound the root into a poultice for sore eyes and dried it for use in a medicine for asthma, bronchitis, and rheumatism.

As the hidden flowers begin to ripen, the spathe withers, and what is left is a cluster of pea-size green berries. By September the berries are bright lacquer-red, beautiful but not edible.

Dogtooth Violet

ERYTHRONIUM AMERICANUM

If you don't know this flower by this name, try trout lily, or yellow adder's tongue, or fawn lily. They are all common names for the same flower. This little, bright yellow lily is tinged brownish-purple on the outside but is clear, unspotted, golden-yellow inside. It has only two leaves, which clasp the stem at the base and are dark green mottled with the same purplish tinge that marks the outside of the flowers. The individual plants grow no more than ten inches high, more often six.

Dogtooth violet, of course, is not even a distant cousin of the ordinary violet. It is a lily, one of the small ones. The names *trout lily* and *fawn lily* come from its time of blooming—late April and May, when trout are biting in the brooks and when does are dropping their fawns in the woodland. The Indians sometimes dug and dried the bulbs and boiled and ate them in winter. But there were other bulbs that gave more return for the labor.

Dogtooth violets mean May Day to me. As a small boy I gathered them for my May baskets, simply because they were one of the few flowers that always were in bloom by then. They didn't keep well, often wilting overnight, but they were beautiful while they lasted.

The plants prefer a damp footing, down along the brook or at the edge of the bog. There is a variety with all-white flowers common only in the West and the South. Its leaves are less mottled, sometimes not mottled at all.

Lilidaceae

Blue Flag

IRIS VERSICOLOR

This is sometimes called larger blue flag because there are several others with smaller flowers or smaller leaves. It will be found in the wet margins of bogs and swamps over much of the United States east of the Rockies. Its flowers resemble the old-fashioned flags of the garden, deep purplish-blue and white, the blue varying in tone from one place to another. Actually, the color is veining over the white background and becomes solid blue only on the margins of the petals. Inside, the petals are yellow at the base.

In some places this is called poison flag because the root contains irisin, a poison so potent that the Indians powdered it, mixed it with animal bile, and dipped their arrow points in the mixture. Anyone even slightly wounded by such arrows, the old reports say, died within a week. But dried, powdered blue flag root was used in many herbal concoctions and regarded as "powerful medicine" for treating stomach cramps and intestinal troubles. The sweet flag that is sometimes candied and regarded as a tasty treat is no relation, not even an iris. Botanically it is *Acorus calamus*, kin of Jack-in-the-pulpit and skunk cabbage.

Among the wild iris tribe is also a southern species called red iris, much like the blue flag except that its flowers are coppery or reddish-brown in color. These two species must be the ancestors of those beautiful old-fashioned garden flags, blue and brown, that I remember seeing in my grandmother's dooryard in eastern Nebraska. By mere chance, we have those same flowers here, given to us by a friend who said they were "just backcountry flags, not really iris."

iridaceae

Wake Robin

TRILLIUM ERECTUM

This trillium is an early flower, usually blooming in April. There are several species of trillium, of which the painted trillium is probably the most beautiful. But all are pretty flowers—on the stem. Please leave this one, the wake robin, right there, on the stem. Another common name for it, and a well-deserved one, is stinking Benjamin. It has the odor of putrid meat. This odor attracts carrion flies, which pollinate the flowers. Some think the color of the flowers helps attract them too, for the three petals are a purplish-red, almost the color of overripe beef.

Wake robin grows best in damp woodlands, and it usually colonizes—find one and you will find a whole community of trilliums. It is three-parted all the way, three rather big, broad, pointed leaves, and three petals on the flower, each petal shaped much like the leaves but much smaller. The flowers are two inches or so across. They mature into berrylike fruits half an inch or so in diameter. The whole plant is seldom more than fifteen inches high, usually nearer twelve.

Another name given this plant is birthwort, and still another is squawroot. Both refer to the use of a decoction of the rootstock as a help during childbirth. The Indians used the plant as an astringent, especially in cases of diarrhea. They also made a poultice of the roots to treat insect and snake bites. And they made a useful salve by chopping and mashing the leaves and adding them to animal fat.

Marsh Marigold

CALTHA PALUSTRIS

You have to get your feet wet to find the biggest and earliest marsh marigolds. They grow in swamps and boglands, by preference, though they are occasionally found on stream margins. But they are worth a wetting, for they are the purest gold that spring provides, a breathtaking golden-yellow.

The flowers are like giant buttercups, the kind that grow in the meadows. The resemblance is no accident, for the swamp marigold belongs to the same family as the buttercup of the meadow—the Latin name means, literally, "marsh cup." However, there is little resemblance between the foliage of the two plants. Marsh marigold leaves are shaped like big violet leaves.

Some call them cowslips, for no understandable reason. The true cowslip belongs to the primrose family and has no resemblance to the marsh marigold. And of all the flowers of spring, only the buttercup itself can rival the marsh marigold in color. Its big, waxy, petal-like sepals are almost as big as a twenty-five-cent piece, however, and dwarf the ordinary buttercup. We eat the leaves as a cooked spring green, one of the best. But they should be cooked before they are eaten. All this family is somewhat poisonous if eaten raw.

The place to find marsh marigolds is where the giant marsh violets grow, preferably where slowly running water warms their roots. The swamp with a slow flow is an ideal place. There marsh marigolds grow in great clumps, on the oozy margins and even in the water itself. There they bloom with a splash of color that can make late April a heart's delight even in a chilly season.

Ranunculaceae

cowslip

Indian Pipe

MONOTROPA UNIFLORA

This is a ghost plant, truly. It has a ghostly color, white or vaguely pink, all the way from root to nodding blossom at its tip. It appears overnight, in the deeper shadows of the woodland, almost as quick in growth as the mushrooms. And it fades overnight, simply withers, blackens, and collapses. Pick one and carry it out into the sunlight and it will have withered and blackened before you've gone a quarter of a mile.

It is a parasite and gets its nourishment from roots and decaying vegetation, always on or near rotting tree trunks. Its stem, which is seldom as much as a foot high, is somewhat scaly and a thick, translucent white. It looks something like a stalk of thoroughly blanched asparagus. The blossom at the tip is the same dead white or slightly pinkish color. It has four, or sometimes five, petals, ten or twelve pale tan stamens. It droops and never opens much. Only rarely is more than one flower seen on a stem. The ovary fattens and assumes an erect position, and it turns a pale grayish-salmon color. It ripens into a fleshy, egg-shaped seed capsule. The seeds are very small and very numerous.

These strange plants grow in clusters, anywhere from three or four to a dozen stems springing from a ball of fibrous rootlets in a mass of rotting wood or other vegetable matter.

You have to go to the deeply shaded woods to discover them, and I find Indian pipe only in late summer, August or even early September.

May Apple

P O D O P H Y L L U M   P E L T A T U M

The May apple is the mandrake of the old herbalists, to which all kinds of powers were ascribed. It was supposed to be a potent love symbol and agent, and it was said to insure pregnancy. It also had a grim aspect in the belief that it seldom grew naturally except under a gallows. But when the root was boiled, an infusion was produced that, it was said, "provoketh sleepe and asswageth paine." Even the smell of the fruit was supposed to produce sleep, though the juice was considered even more effective.

It is a rather handsome plant, with two big leaves at the top of each divided stalk, the leaves unusual because their deeply divided sections spread like an umbrella, supported by the stem in the center. The blossom, a white, six-petaled flower often two inches across, droops from a short stem between the two leaf stalks. The blossom is pretty but unpleasant in odor. It has no nectar, but bumblebees collect its pollen and cross-fertilize it. The blossom ripens into a lemon-shaped fruit an inch or two long, which, though full of seeds, is edible. It has a lemony taste.

The May apples are not found in most of New England, though they do grow in lower Connecticut and from there west and south. In a painful time of my life I went often to a wooded hillside where May apples grew by the hundreds, and I thought the sourness of their fruit had a symbolism for me. Instead, I was to find both love and happiness soon thereafter. So to me it is the mandrake, the love symbol, of the old dealers in plant restoratives.

Berberidaceae

Yellow Lady's-Slipper

CYPRIPEDIUM CALCEOLUS

This isn't the largest or the rarest of the lady's-slippers, but I think it is one of the most beautiful. The color of its blossoms is as clean and bright a yellow as I ever see, a golden-yellow just touched with fine striping of madder-purple. And there may be three or four blossoms on the same plant, one above another. The stem is clasped by the warm green leaves and often grows as much as two feet tall. It prefers the half-shade of woodland borders, and it doesn't normally choose bogland. One of the most beautiful plants I know grows on a steep hillside above a lake, two-thirds of the way up the hill and at the foot of a rock ledge, where it is well watered but also well drained.

The generic name comes from *Kypris,* the Greek name for Venus, and *podion,* for slipper. So the common name is a literal translation—or the other way around, actually; the botanical name was taken from the common name. The specific name is somewhat redundant, *calceolus* meaning "a small shoe." The blossoms are somewhat smaller than those of the common pink moccasin flower.

Some prefer the showy lady's-slipper to this one; it has white blossoms marked with light crimson-magenta and, as its name says, it is a showy flower. It demands attention. But my choice among all the lady's-slippers is this yellow one, for grace, for color, and for total beauty. The old herbalists made a brew of its root and administered it for sleeplessness.

orchid

Rue Anemone

There are two of these small, white-flowered anemones, both blooming very early. One, the wood anemone, has deep green leaves in
five sharp-pointed divisions. The other, the one we show here, is the
rue anemone, whose leaves are olive green and somewhat resemble
those of wild columbine, being rounded and in vaguely defined large
lobes. The rue anemone's flowers come in a cluster of two to five
flowers, each on its own thin stem, at the tip of the leaf stalk.

The name, both common and scientific, simply means wind
flower, with the same Greek root as the word *anemometer*. It is believed by some, and was said by the ancients, that the anemones
never open flower until the gentle winds of spring blow. I wouldn't
for the world dispute this, but the fact is that these dainty flowers
also open wide on a clear, sunny, altogether calm April day.

The early English herbalists seem to have made no use of the
anemones, though they did suggest that sniffing the juice would
"purge the head." American Indians, however, considered the
anemone a powerful agent for good. Just to see anemones was a
favorable sign. They believed the roots were potent enough to cure
such a stubborn affliction as lockjaw, and they thought that anemone
tea and a bath of anemone decoction would cure, or at least arrest,
leprosy.

Trailing Arbutus

E P I G A E A   R E P E N S

The arbutus is one of the heaths, cousin of checkerberry, mountain laurel, and pinxter. But the arbutus is a creeper, never lifting a leaf more than a foot off the ground. It blooms early and is also known as the Mayflower, named for the month, not the ship.

A good many New Englanders think arbutus fragrance is the sweetest on Earth. I doubt that they are the ones, however, who almost loved the flower to death a generation ago by picking it and pulling it up by the roots. Trailing arbutus doesn't transplant readily and doesn't make much of a display as a cut flower, but people kept right on plucking it and digging it until laws were passed to protect the plant. That helped, but it was belated action. Besides, every time a new expressway was cut through the woods, which seems to be the chosen place for any six-lane highway, more native habitat for arbutus was destroyed. So today only the really dedicated seeker can find arbutus; and when he or she finds it, the place becomes both sacred and secret. Thus we may yet preserve a few native growths of trailing arbutus.

I know of four or five places where arbutus still grows, but I wouldn't tell my own grandchildren. The blossoms are tubular with five lobes, white or pink-tinged, and have a kind of frosty look. They are small, no more than half an inch across, but they bloom in clusters. Early queen bumblebees visit them for nectar to feed their first broods.

The botanical name is redundant. *Epigaea* is from the Greek words for "upon the earth," and *repens* is from the Latin for "lying on the ground."

Jewelweed

IMPATIENS CAPENSIS

Give it half a chance and jewelweed will take over almost any damp, woodsy spot. Its tall, bright green stems and leaves, almost translucent in the sunlight, make a small jungle. But walk through it and you leave a clear path, for those stems have all the brittle frailty of any succulent plant. Break them and they ooze juice, which country boys declare is a cure for ivy poisoning. It works for my neighbors, and it may for you. I happen to be immune.

Seen in the morning sunlight, a patch of jewelweed seems to gleam with orange-yellow spangles. Look more closely and you find the flowers that give the plant its common name. Strange flowers, with a deep, saclike base and the petals joined in a bell-shaped form with divided lobes, the whole a rich golden-yellow, almost bronze, and speckled like a robin's egg, the speckles a brownish-red. The flowers are small and fragile, and they hang from slender stems. Bees seek them out, and quite a few hummingbirds come to suck nectar from their depths.

Touch-me-not, the plant is sometimes called, because when the flowers are gone and the pods ripen, an inner tension is established which pops those seeds as from a miniature catapult if any passerby should brush against them. Thus does the jewelweed spread so swiftly—it hurls its seeds in all directions, profligate and persistent. Botanically it belongs to the family called Balsaminaceae, and it is close kin to the cultivated flower known as balsam or, erroneously, as lady's-slipper, which adds its fragrance and varicolored beauty to the old-fashioned garden. But jewelweed is no cutting flower, even for those who would bring wildlings indoors. It is largely foliage anyway. Its jewels are small and best seen in the damp woodland by those willing to go there before the morning dew has dried.

Dutchman's Breeches

DICENTRA CUCULLARIA

Dutchman's breeches bloom on stony hillsides where the sun of late April has begun to warm the soil beneath the leafless trees. The little white breeks tipped with yellow sway on their slender stems, and the gray-green foliage feathers out around them as graceful as fresh fern fronds.

There is a dainty grace about Dutchman's breeches, both in flower and leaf, that is matched among the early spring flowers only by the anemones. And the anemones seem fragile; they lack the jaunty air of the breeks, which, although they quickly wither when picked, give the appearance of being firmly rooted and able to stand up to anything that April brings.

Botanists call them *Dicentra cucullaria*, from the Greek which means double-spurred. The reference is to the flower's shape. Actually, it has four petals. Two of them are joined to make the somewhat heart-shaped sac, which is technically double-spurred. The other two petals are inside the sac, very small and designed to protect the stamens. If you seem to see a resemblance to the garden flower called bleeding heart, it is no illusion. They are cousins.

The shape of the Dutchman's breeches flower makes it a natural host to the early bees, particularly the bumblebees, which are the chief agents of cross-fertilization. Honeybees visit the breeks, but they can't quite reach the nectar. Early butterflies also find a welcome.

In another month squirrel corn, *Dicentra canadensis*, a close cousin of Dutchman's breeches, will be in bloom on the same banks. But just now it's the season for the breeks themselves, jaunty as any boy in freshly laundered pantaloons.

Joe-Pye-Weed

E U P A T O R I U M   F I S T U L O S U M

If the shade of old Joe Pye isn't out in the morning mists of late August surveying the crop of wild herbs at the pasture margin and down by the cattail swamp, he is missing the chance of his afterlife. His namesake plant is in full bloom by late August in the lowlands, magenta-red and eye-catching. Nearby are its cousins, boneset and thoroughwort, and over at the edge of the woodland is the snow-white froth of snakeroot, still another cousin, with a special richness of blossom.

Joe Pye was a "yarb man," an Indian with special skills who made the rounds of rural New England years ago and seems to have been a specialist in reducing fevers. Beyond that, little is known of him, though tavern records in Stockbridge, Massachusetts, in the 1770s show that he bought rum there. Rum was an ingredient of a good many potions the herb doctors used. Even Joe Pye's birth and death dates are unknown. But he is one of the very few herb doctors who ever had a plant named after him. We still call it Joe-Pye-weed, and it has no other common name.

Its botanical name honors Eupator Mithradates, emperor of Pontus and ruler of Asia Minor in the first century B.C. He was said to have used one species of the plant, which also grows in eastern Europe and Africa, in medicine. This plant, either dried or fresh, has a sweetly vanilla-scented odor when bruised or pounded. The upper leaves are tinged with purple even before the flowers bloom.

Baneberry

ACTAEA RUBRA

There are two baneberries very much alike except that one has red berries and the other white ones—usually. *Actaea rubra* has the red berries, deep cranberry red. *Actaea pachypoda* has the white berries, often called doll's eyes because they are china white with a dark spot or "pupil," like the eyes of small dolls. But now and then *Actaea rubra* has white berries and *Actaea pachypoda* has red berries; sports or freaks, but very puzzling.

Baneberries bloom early, by late April in my area. The blossoms, very small and white, look almost like a puff of mist, a round puff on the red variety, an oval puff on the white. They are pollinated by small flies and bees. They have pollen but no nectar. A little later the pea-size berries form in a cluster at the stem tip, the red ones in a rather tight, round cluster, the white ones in a looser, longer cluster.

The berries may look edible, but they are poisonous. They cause heart disturbance as well as intestinal trouble. The rootstock produces extreme purgative and emetic effects. But so far as I can learn, nobody ever died from baneberry poisoning, possibly because its berries and roots have an unpleasant taste.

As blossoms, the baneberry flowers are delicately beautiful. They appear almost as soon as the plant has leafed out. They are borne on bright red stems. Something must eat those berries, birds or small animals, though I have never seen it happen. All I know is that they ripen and disappear.

There is a large western variety, with red berries, actually a small shrub, that grows from Nebraska westward.

Ranunculaceae

Wild Blue Phlox

PHLOX DIVARICATA

This is the only wild phlox that grows in my area, and I cherish it. Some guides call its flowers lilac or pale violet, but those I know are a good true blue, almost a chicory color.

The name *Phlox* comes from the Greek word for flame, and the *divaricata* is from the Latin word meaning divergent or branched. It refers to the plant's way of branching at the top so that it bears several clusters of flowers. I have never heard it called by any special common name. It grows from western Connecticut across New York state and on west at least as far as Minnesota, and it prefers the edges of moist woodlands. I have never seen a plant that grew more than a foot and a half tall. Some people bring it into their flower gardens and coddle it, but special treatment seems to make no particular difference—it remains about the same height, blooms about the same time and no more generously. It does make a more easily managed plant, however, than the tall, tame phlox, and it never reverts to that unhappy magenta shade that seems to be the ultimate color of all tame phlox let go to seed.

The Indians—and inevitably those pioneers who picked up herbal lore from their Indian neighbors—used this phlox in herbal medicine. The whole plant was boiled to make a tea that was a kind of all-purpose dose for bellyache, constipation, and diarrhea. The roots were steeped to make an eyewash, and the boiled roots were believed useful in fighting venereal disease.

Wood Sorrel

OXALIS MONTANA

At a glance, these dainty little plants may be mistaken for the everyday white clover that grows in our dooryard grass. Their threefold leaves are shaped like clover leaves, though they often are indented at the tips. But the flowers are a giveaway—they bear no resemblance to clover blossoms. They are five-petaled with smooth, round petals, and in most species they are warm golden-yellow. This species, however, has white petals with pink or crimson lines in them; and another species, common only in the South, has pale magenta petals.

The white-petaled species is sometimes called wood shamrock. All wood sorrels actually resemble the Irish shamrock, to which they are related. The species most common where I live is the yellow wood sorrel, sometimes called lady's sorrel, sometimes plain everyday oxalis. It is a persistent but not an obnoxious weed in fields and gardens.

The sorrels are rich in vitamin C. Long before vitamins were discovered and named, though, sorrel was used by discerning people as a slightly acid green to be eaten raw in a salad, in cooked greens, in soup, or with eggs. The American Indians ate it whenever they could find it and considered it the best of all treatments for the "winter sickness," which we now know was scurvy. The Indians used it in many ways, including a sorrel drink that tasted much like lemonade.

Some sorrels are purple on the underside of the leaves, and on cloudy days the leaves fold shut, like butterfly wings. Come across a patch of it this way in a woodland and it is like a purple shadow come down to earth.

Index of Common Names

Index of Scientific Names

Les Line has been the editor of *Audubon*, the magazine of the National Audubon Society, since 1966. He is also a noted nature photographer, and his pictures have appeared in many books and national magazines. His byline, as photographer, editor, or author, appears on eighteen books. In 1981, he was awarded an honorary degree of Doctor of Literature from Bucknell University. Born in Sparta, Michigan, Les Line began his journalism career at the age of twelve, writing sports stories and taking pictures for local newspapers. As a reporter in Midland, Michigan, he won many awards for news photography and conservation writing. Mr. Line lives with his wife and two children in Dobbs Ferry, New York. They have a country retreat in Dutchess County, "just over the hills" from the Borland farm in adjacent Connecticut.

Hal Borland was born in Nebraska, grew up in Colorado, and lived in New England from 1945 until his death in 1978. He is the author of more than thirty books—including the classic *When the Legends Die,* his memoirs, *High, Wide and Lonesome,* and two recent favorites, *Hal Borland's Book of Days* and *Hal Borland's Twelve Moons of the Year.* He was for many years a contributing editor of *Audubon* magazine. In 1942, he wrote the first of the "outdoor editorials" that became an institution in the Sunday edition of *The New York Times.* Mr. Borland received many honors and awards, among them the John Burroughs Nature Award in 1968 for *Hill Country Harvest.* His wife, author Barbara Dodge Borland, still lives on their 100-acre Connecticut farm beside the Housatonic River in the lower Berkshires.

A Note on the Type

The text of this book was set in Weiss, a typeface designed in Germany by Emil Rudolf Weiss (1875–1942). The design of the roman was completed in 1928 and that of the italic in 1931. Both are well balanced and even in color, reflecting the subtle skill of a fine calligrapher.

Composition by American–Stratford Graphic Services, Inc., Brattleboro, Vermont. Separations by Chanticleer Press, Inc., New York, New York. Printing by Rae Publishing Company, Cedar Grove, New Jersey. Binding by American Book–Stratford Press, Saddle Brook, New Jersey.

Design by Dorothy Schmiderer